Process Driven Comprehensive Auditing

Also available from ASQ Quality Press:

The Process-Focused Organization: A Transition Strategy for Success
Robert A. Gardner

The Process Auditing Techniques Guide
J. P. Russell

The Internal Auditing Pocket Guide
J. P. Russell

How to Audit the Process-Based QMS
Dennis R. Arter, Charles A. Cianfrani, and John E. (Jack) West

ISO Lesson Guide 2000: Pocket Guide to Q9001:2000, 2nd Edition
Dennis R. Arter and J. P. Russell.

Quality Audit Handbook, 2nd Edition
ASQ Quality Audit Division

Quality Audits for Improved Performance, 3rd Edition
Dennis R. Arter

The ISO 9001:2000 Auditor's Companion
Kent A. Keeney

To request a complimentary catalog of ASQ Quality Press publications,
call 800-248-1946, or visit our Web site at http://qualitypress.asq.org.

Process Driven Comprehensive Auditing

A New Way to Conduct
ISO 9001:2000 Internal Audits

Paul C. Palmes

ASQ Quality Press
Milwaukee, Wisconsin

American Society for Quality, Quality Press, Milwaukee 53203
© 2005 by American Society for Quality
All rights reserved. Published 2004
Printed in the United States of America

12 11 10 09 08 07 06 05 04   5 4 3 2 1

Library of Congress Cataloging-in-Publication Data

Palmes, Paul C., 1948–
    Process driven comprehensive auditing : a new way to conduct ISO 9001:2000
    internal audits / Paul C. Palmes.
        p. cm.
    Includes index.
    ISBN 0-87389-641-6 (soft cover)
    1. Auditing, Internal—Quality control.   2. Total quality management—
    Measurement.   3. ISO 9001 Standard.   I. Title.

    HF5668.25P352   2005
    657'.458—dc22   2004021391

ISBN 0-87389-641-6

Publisher: William A. Tony
Acquisitions Editor: Annemieke Hytinen
Project Editor: Paul O'Mara
Production Administrator: Randall Benson
Special Marketing Representative: David Luth

ASQ Mission: The American Society for Quality advances individual,
organizational, and community excellence worldwide through learning, quality
improvement, and knowledge exchange.

Attention Bookstores, Wholesalers, Schools, and Corporations: ASQ Quality Press
books, videotapes, audiotapes, and software are available at quantity discounts with
bulk purchases for business, educational, or instructional use. For information,
please contact ASQ Quality Press at 800-248-1946, or write to ASQ Quality Press,
P.O. Box 3005, Milwaukee, WI 53201-3005.

To place orders or to request a free copy of
the ASQ Quality Press Publications Catalog,
including ASQ membership information,
call 800-248-1946. Visit our Web site at
www.asq.org or http://qualitypress.asq.org.

Quality Press
600 N. Plankinton Avenue
Milwaukee, Wisconsin 53203
Call toll free 800-248-1946
Fax 414-272-1734
www.asq.org
http://qualitypress.asq.org
http://standardsgroup.asq.org
E-mail: authors@asq.org

∞ Printed on acid-free paper

Contents

Preface

This book was written for the novice internal auditor. The goal is to provide an easy-to-understand method for conducting a highly effective audit. The quality community today is confused about the proper approach to "process auditing," and auditor training hasn't yet discovered a simple technique to educate and train new auditors. Instead, most auditor training programs are still little more than a continuation of past programs that were confusing, bewildering, and often irrelevant to students.

In almost 19 years of experience in the quality profession, it has been my observation that most internal auditors are rank-and-file workers in their organizations. Plant workers, maintenance staff, and occasional office members make up the average list of internal auditors in most companies. Though typically not drawn from the quality department, they begin their experience as new auditors trying to grapple with the details and subtleties of their quality management system, or QMS. In fact, most 16-hour internal auditor training programs spend the greater part of the first day explaining and examining the QMS, much to the confusion and frustration of students not normally accustomed to quickly digesting such concentrated and detailed information. Adding insult to injury, the second day is often a role-play exercise in which the new student is asked to prepare a mock audit of a fictitious company whose issues are of comic book proportions. From this exercise, the formerly frustrated student is somehow supposed to be transformed into a qualified auditor, ready to face the real world of internal auditing.

Unfortunately, this approach does not work satisfactorily and is often quite counterproductive, because of the following realities:

- Traditional auditor training is devoted to compliance, not process auditing techniques. Until now, an easy-to-understand process auditing model has been a remote and difficult concept to teach.

- Auditor training that concentrates first on the elements of the ISO 9001:2000 Standard is destined to intimidate, not empower, the novice auditor. Faced with a mountain of carefully worded and technical-sounding information, the thrill of volunteering is quickly replaced by other less expansive emotions—namely fatigue, helplessness, and frustration. None of these feelings is conducive to learning.

- Auditors are typically chosen from the most inquisitive, bright, and responsible people within the organization. They deserve an approach that appeals to these positive traits, rather than forcing them to essentially memorize a bewildering amount of information before they can apply any of it as auditors. Worst of all is training that essentially convinces them that they will never grasp the foundational information, followed by meaningless exercises that are only marginally representative of real-life conditions.

Process Driven Comprehensive Auditing takes a new approach, one that affirms the student's willingness to learn and contribute to the company as an internal auditor by simplifying a complex series of actions. It does this through examination and guided application of Shewhart and Deming's "PDCA cycle." PDCA—the acronym for Plan, Do, Check, Act—is at the foundation of the ISO 9001:2000 Standard, but until now has been relegated to second-tier status as a basic auditing approach. However, the power of PDCA is first and foremost its ability to be easily understood. When harnessed to the task of training new auditors, PDCA provides an easy-to-follow and consistent model for true process auditing. Process Driven Comprehensive Auditing takes more than its name from the letters of the PDCA cycle. Comprehensiveness is vital to excellence in auditing, and PDCA is a comprehensive approach to improvement of any process.

By combining a series of general questions drawn from many elements of the ISO 9001:2000 Standard with a cross-reference guide to particular elements such as Purchasing, Design, Production Control, and Calibration, the methods presented in this book offer a practical and uncomplicated starting point for the first-time auditor. Those who have already adopted this approach overwhelmingly find it to be superior to past methods, not only for the simplicity of its design, but also because the auditor is not focused first and foremost on compliance to the ISO 9001:2000 Standard. Instead, the new auditor begins the examination of process performance by asking a simple question from which all others eventually follow.

The lack of real value in many internal auditing programs has been an alarming and unfortunate outgrowth of the obsession to adhere to "the letter" rather than the substance and intent of an organization's QMS. Whether a particular *i* is dotted or whether all purchase orders are signed has marginal value compared to the discovery of a major improvement as the result of a meaningful audit. Evidence of plans and activities that simply parallel elements of the ISO 9001:2000 Standard have their place. However, evidence of those same elements at work within the organization coupled to analysis and improvement planning has far more significance to top management, as well as lasting sustainability. The Process Driven Comprehensive Auditing approach is designed to find and report process excellence as well as weaknesses to accomplish this objective.

PDCA was chosen by the authors of the ISO 9001:2000 Standard because it offers a road map to continuous improvement. Little wonder that it is also a road map to conducting a readily understood and continuously improving internal audit program. First-time auditors need all the help they can get. What follows is a sincere attempt to provide them and the companies they work for with an opportunity to realize success quickly, regardless of their prior experience as auditors or knowledge of their particular QMS.

Acknowledgments

This book was inspired by a dinner conversation with Janine Johnson, midwest regional manager for CRS Registrars. As we talked, it became clear that we were as interested in the potential of the 2000 revision of ISO 9001 as we were distressed by the lack of innovation and attention to internal auditor training.

There had to be a better way! Months later, in a hotel room overlooking the Seattle skyline, the answer came as a sudden insight: The process approach and PDCA, described one after the other in the standard, can also link together as a tool to easily teach anyone to perform a true process audit!

Thanks, Janine. From that moment to this, I have many to thank for the completion of this project. To my colleagues in US TC 176 who offered encouragement, especially Dan Harper and J. P. Russell, and ASQ Quality Press's Paul O'Mara and Annemieke Hytinen, my sincerest thanks! My colleagues in ISO SC3, WG 11—Switzerland's Tommie Johansson, Gordon Hawley of the UK, our own Denise Robitaille, and Australia's Kevin Foley—also deserve special mention as early supporters and sage advisers in discussions of PDCA from Bucharest to Sydney.

Wayne Voorhees, whose only wish for each of his employees is that we reach for our dreams, deserves special mention as an exemplary Level 5 leader. His support and encouragement, along with my fellow "Northern Pipers," especially Kristin Munro and all the good people at Otter Tail Corporation, sustained me in more ways than one over the past several years.

And to the Pegster, always willing to listen, read, edit, and advise throughout the life of this project, I am most grateful. Most wives accept a certain amount of separation from time to time, but being miles away is also possible in the same room when the next chapter calls. Love and thanks from deep inside!

I've read hundreds of acknowledgments in as many books, and they all seem to conclude with the same admission of failure: the impossibility of including all the people who've contributed to and supported the effort it takes to complete this sort of project. However, I've not yet read one that included you, the reader. This project will be complete when you've finished your first true process audit. It will soon be you I wish to thank most of all for the ultimate completion of this work, as you give life to a new methodology that grew in response to an impassioned dinner conversation.

Finally, for all this to have amazingly come together affirms a wonderful truth, a special life force: There are no coincidences. Thanks to the Spirit that awakens and nurtures the unlimited possibilities in us all.

1

The Auditor's Journey

A journey of a thousand miles must begin with a single step.

—Lao-tzu (604–531 B.C.), The Way of Lao-tzu

The ISO 9001:2000 quality management standard recognizes that the first step is, contrary to popular thought, not the beginning of the journey. The 2000 revision makes clear that in a world-class organization, taking the first step is actually the *second* occurrence. In fact, as the degree of risk increases, the design of the standard helps organizations to proceed with caution, to think about what they intend to do, and perhaps to test their assumptions before actually taking that decisive first step.

Steven Covey, in his book *The 7 Habits of Highly Effective People,* calls the true first step in any journey "the first creation." We think about what we're going to do, where we're going, and all the other issues we'll need to consider before beginning most things in life. The first creation is simply a thought—it's in the mind. It's the artist's vision of what a painting will be long before the first brushstroke meets canvas. The first creation is the idea, the thought, the inspiration, and the plan to make it happen.

The plan comes first; the "journey" is actually decided before taking that first step. In modern-day business language, the true first step is often one or more planning meetings. Action items, the typical next step, are the things that must get done after those meetings. The 2000 revision of the ISO 9001 standard places a great deal of emphasis on planning in an effort to guide the organization away from rushing into action without considering all the issues. In other words, think about what's involved before making any journey, regardless of the distance.

Planning is not only good quality practice, it's also good business practice. If an organization plans well and acts accordingly, the odds of success are quite good. High quality and good business are related, and the ISO 9001:2000 Standard's emphasis on customer focus and involvement of top management relies on involving both these entities in the planning

1

process. After all, top management is in charge of business planning decisions, and customers are the ones who buy and use the things that result from all that planning. So, because business and quality both rely on and succeed through effective planning, world-class operations are characteristically eager to continuously seek improvements to those plans.

The internal auditing element of the 2000 revision of the ISO 9001 standard mentions the words *planned* or *planning* four times. Not only is a documented audit process plan necessary, but the planned length of time between audits and the planning requirements of the quality management system itself must also be built into the scope of internal audits. The standard requires auditors not just to examine what an organization does, but also to investigate the planning designed to get the job done. This is an important point, because while most would assume that auditing is essentially determining whether people are doing their work according to some plan, the standard is now pointing out that the plan itself is as important as the things people do.

COMPLIANCE AUDITS VERSUS THE PDCA APPROACH

Once again, we see that it's essential to take time to plan before acting. However, traditional internal auditing typically examines more of what's actually done within an organization instead of the plan designed to do it. This approach is often called *compliance auditing*. The auditor carefully examines what's happening and compares those activities to the appropriate elements within the standard. The only real value to this approach is to determine whether the organization is or isn't acting within narrowly defined guidelines.

For example, an auditor might ask, "Is there a calibration program in place, and are there records of calibrated equipment?" The typical answer to both parts of that question is yes. Of course, we've learned nothing about the overall calibration plan, and even less about whether it's being measured and found to be working effectively. The same goes for all the other elements calling for particular tools to be in place or specific processes to be documented. Some call these "the shalls." Throughout the ISO 9001:2000 Standard, the phrase "the organization shall" appears many times. Compliance auditing looks for each of these "shalls" and essentially uses them as a yes/no checklist.

In another example, the standard makes clear that the organization must explain its auditing process in a documented procedure and that the audit criteria, scope, frequency, and methods be defined. With these requirements in mind, a compliance audit first investigates whether the audit process has been documented. Once again, this is a yes/no issue. Next, the auditor examines the document itself to determine whether it addresses "audit criteria." This also yields a yes/no answer, as the audit criteria either are or are not explained in the process. On and on we go through audit scope, frequency, and methods—each time asking simply, "Are these defined in the written process?" Assuming the answer is yes to all the above, the auditor is free to move on to the next set of "shalls" to make the appropriate judgments, each in isolation having relatively little importance or impact on the ability of the organization to improve.

Compliance auditing is easy to teach, easy to monitor, and easy to discount in organizations that are searching for real opportunities to improve. Too often, corrective, disciplinary follow-up is about all that takes place in the aftermath of a compliance audit. Having found a break in the system, corrective action is implied as a necessity, regardless of the significance of the infraction. Tedious findings devalue the entire process of auditing and its reputation as a tool for improvement is tarnished.

World-class companies need more than the typical output of compliance auditing to make real interactive and meaningful improvements. They need internal audits that tell a complete story, not just what is or isn't compliant to the standard.

PDCA (Plan, Do, Check, Act) auditing satisfies this need by looking at individual processes within organizations as links in a chain, each dependent on the other, each with its own plan to minimize risk and to do the best work possible.

Whereas compliance auditing first asks whether the company adheres to ISO 9001:2000 requirements, the first step of PDCA auditing is to look instead at the organization. Unlike compliance auditing, the PDCA approach is designed to first determine whether the process under examination is working as planned to satisfy the needs of the organization and its customers. The beauty of this approach is that if the process truly is performing as planned and meeting customers' needs, then it must also be in compliance with important ISO requirements as well.

Once a specific area is identified, the audit team designs an audit that first examines the established plan to manage risks in that area. With the standard's strong attention to planning, many of these elements are brought into the audit at this stage. Remember that the plan itself is as important as the things people do. But unique to PDCA auditing is that these same planning elements apply to multiple areas within an organization. The PDCA approach recognizes that to some extent every department within the organization develops a plan to do its work. For the internal auditor, this means the organization can now use the same basic set of planning questions in each of its audits and thereby continually monitor planning within its operating system.

The same condition exists within each of the remaining three phases of a PDCA audit: doing, checking, and acting. Within each of these phases the auditor uses a generic list of questions—drawn from throughout the ISO 9001:2000 Standard—that applies to any area under examination. This approach helps beginning and advanced auditors to conduct each audit with greater confidence and assurance that their work will include more than one or two of the PDCA elements within the area they inspect. And most importantly, the essence of PDCA auditing is that the auditor now follows the natural progression of planning: taking those first steps, checking the terrain, and finally embarking on the journey.

PDCA auditing goes well beyond the "shalls." It guides the auditor through the process of investigating the strength of a crucial link in the organization's chain—the link that recognizes a customer's needs and then provides products to satisfy them.

MEET YOUR CUSTOMER: TOP MANAGEMENT

As a business system, the health and safety of ISO 9001:2000 implementation within an organization is, or certainly should be, a prime concern of top management. As auditors, we work within this system—probing, inspecting, and reporting on its performance. If one or more processes are weak or ineffective, the system will also be weak and ineffective. Auditors are process examiners, interested in process planning, safety, and effectiveness. Top management needs thorough examiners to bring them solid information to make the best decisions.

If the system is weak, if processes are unreliable, silos will almost surely be in place—well staffed and protected. Silo departments can be team players, but only within their unique unit. They are often highly protective. They're not members of an interconnected and interdependent chain because they've learned the hard way that others within the organization are not dependable. When top management is insulated from these pockets of self-interest, or simply fails to lead, leadership falls to the silo masters. Then, instead of everyone working for a common outcome, each department works for its own outcome. That's not good business—and once again, top management needs solid data to make the necessary improvements. Using PDCA auditing methods, internal auditors can and should provide this valuable information.

According to the ISO 9001:2000 Standard, top management is first directed to clearly provide strategic direction in the form of a quality policy and stated objectives. Then, they must define the *system,* the series of processes that are required to carry out those objectives in order to achieve the quality policy. Now if every department, no matter what specific work it does, is attempting to accomplish its share of whatever it takes to achieve these objectives, they should all be working toward those common goals.

To an auditor, silos are an indication that top management's quality policy and objectives need attention and strengthening. After all, they are the vision and guiding spirit of the company. Together, they are the big plan to make it all happen. And without majority involvement, a steady stream of concentration, understanding, and participation, improvements will be slow in coming.

Once they've defined the system, top management is committed. After all, why would they invest their time and energy to plan and put together a system only to walk away from the actual journey? The odds are poor that rational businesspeople would invest in developing what they believe is a winning system and then abandon it for lack of confidence or a steadfast belief in their handiwork. Throughout the standard, top management is singled out as "responsible" to plan, do, check, and act on information generated by the system they themselves defined. Change the phrase *management responsibility* to *management commitment and involvement* and the difference between the old and the new standard is clear. This time ISO is a business tool, invaluable to the company to manage its most important affairs. PDCA auditing brings the entire process of planning, implementation, measurement, and improvement to the attention of the people most in need of this information.

> **Note:** Perhaps your experience as an auditor or quality professional brings you to wonder how a new approach to auditing can have direct application for top management within your organization. It's entirely possible that in certain settings internal audits are regarded as a limited quality department function. But the PDCA difference is in its approach. Instead of compliance steeped in ISO processes, language, and requirements, the PDCA auditor examines your company's processes directly, bringing ISO into the discussion only when it helps to explain best practices. The PDCA auditing approach is very user-friendly to top management because it can be such a valuable tool. As you read through this book, give thought to how often top management would be grateful to learn of process management problems, resource control issues, and many of the important operational measurements that indicate progress or problems within your organization.

THE CUSTOMER CONNECTION

Top management's objective is simple: Sell to or service more customers. And little could be as basic as the relationship between suppliers and customers in one fundamental aspect: Both want more. And because each must know what the other requires, it's obvious that making product in a primarily inward-focused system is the opposite of what's necessary to achieve success. However, an amazing number of businesses and service organizations continue to listen more to themselves than to their customers. The cost of this misdirection is the internal use of energy that would otherwise be made stronger through positive feedback from a loyal and growing customer base. It is customer feedback that confirms the value of a day's work and the leadership that created the system to make it all happen.

The ISO 9001:2000 Standard understands that building loyalty and a positive market presence requires a plan that first seeks to understand what customers want, then to design operations to produce it, and finally to deliver it as efficiently as possible. Put simply, ISO is actually a business plan built to give the customer what he or she wants. As auditors, we are therefore looking for a system designed and monitored by top management, and built to satisfy the customer. This "customer connection" is something that auditors must be sensitive to and watch for as they go about their work, regardless of the area under investigation.

A strong and successful organization will have that customer connection. Each department will have it. Work will be directed to getting more and more of it, and all information that helps to better understand the customer will be welcomed, analyzed, and incorporated into the company's product or service. A strong customer connection balances internal thinking against external concerns. Organizations whose system is dedicated to strengthening the link between themselves and their customers make improvements based on what their customers want. They look outward for their customers' reactions to their products and then make changes within the company, redirecting their work to provide more of what the customer requires. Their common goal is customer satisfaction, something departments should be working together to achieve, according to top management objectives. The PDCA audit system is designed to search for this customer connection—and, once again, it all starts with Covey's "first creation": the plan.

TOP MANAGEMENT AND STRATEGIC RISK PLANNING

We know that top management's overall strategic plan should be customer based. We also know that this plan is something we should recognize wherever we are in the organization, and if it's working we should see increased customer satisfaction levels. This information could be from many possible sources: direct customer surveys, sales reports, industry reports and surveys, shipping or installation summary reports, and service center reports or logs. A complete list is unnecessary; each organization will have its own description of how it monitors and learns about its customers. Just ask.

Now, take a moment to ask yourself why all this is important in the first place. Sure, making products without knowing what the customer wants is silly. However, there's a lot more going on than being kind to the hand that feeds you. Every business owner knows that one major mistake could mean sending everyone home and closing the doors. The bottom line to the whole idea of turning customer needs into well-managed processes is to find a reliable way to control risk.

Controlling risk is what top management does all day, every day. Their work is to make decisions to best distribute money to pay for staff, machinery, buildings, and all the other things that require funding. They rarely call their work *money management,* perhaps because it sounds more like something routinely carried out by the finance department. *Resource management* is the more popular term, but it's still money and they are the ones who make the decisions about who or what gets it, and how much.

Those decisions are easier to make when it's clear that an investment will deliver a return. The more obvious it is to invest, the less risk of wasting money. PDCA audits are an excellent way to determine whether investments in processes are actually performing as expected.

THE VIEW FROM THE TOP

I once spoke to a group of top managers—company presidents and CEOs. As I drove to the meeting, I found myself searching for the perfect approach to address them as a group. I was told beforehand that these dozen or so business leaders were at various stages in the process of developing their strategic plans, many for the second or third time in their company's history. I wanted to find common ground quickly between them and the topic, which was essentially quality as good business, so I tried to imagine how each one managed daily decisions.

Knowing that a well-designed quality system should provide top management with a wealth of information vital to making good decisions, I decided to begin by asking how many of these business leaders relied mostly on reports and conversations with others to make decisions. As expected, they all shared a strong dependence on their management group to provide them with most of the information they used to make decisions.

I next asked them to take a minute to consider what was at stake in regard to most decisions they made on the basis of input from others. As discussed earlier, there is a very basic and universal answer to that question. It took awhile, but eventually they all agreed that their number one job was to control risk through decisions about where, when, and how to spend money.

And because all these decisions were based on information supplied by systems and people other than themselves, it made great sense to be surrounded by very good systems and people who are good at what they do. In addition, everyone agreed that the risk of making a bad decision decreased in direct proportion to the amount of good information they received.

I wrote the following on the conference room board:

1. Top management's job is to make decisions.

2. Decisions are based primarily on information supplied to top managers.

3. The better the information, the better the decision.

4. Top management decisions are about minimizing risk.

5. Risk is managed through decisions about the best use of resources.

6. Good resource management is good risk management.

"So," I asked, "how many are surrounded by the best information to make possible the very best decision about where to invest the company's resources in order to control risk?"

Of course, almost everyone believed that their management group was exceptional and that they routinely received great information on a regular basis. Not willing to let them off the hook, I pressed the issue of what exactly they considered to be great information, and without exception they spoke of solid reports and conversations about their operational issues, their internally focused concerns.

"If risk management is the goal," I said, carefully setting the hook, "and internal information drives your decisions, it appears as though you are primarily making decisions about how to protect yourself from yourself!" In other words, all the efficiency and financial reports, all the project status meetings, and all the budget reviews that normally consume the majority of top management's time represent information growing out of internal goals and measurements brought to them by their trusted top insiders.

Because the greatest risk to any service provider or producer is to operate in a manner that alienates or forgets its customers, top managers need information from outside the organization, not just from the closely knit management group that typically surrounds them. Armed with solid information about what is or isn't acceptable from the customer perspective, top managers can then work with their staff to decide on a plan that allocates resources to produce products or services that customers want. Without this vital information, the risk of making poor decisions is almost assured.

I looked around the room and knew I had made the point. Top management's strategic plan has to begin with a thorough understanding of their customers and their market. Once that concept was in place, the rest of my presentation was fairly straightforward: "If you know what customers want, the next step is to create a plan to get it to them."

As auditors, we are always looking for plans or processes that can be traced directly to a decision to do things a certain way based on the greater risk to the company if it were done differently. And the fundamental risk is the possibility that the customer would not accept the product or service the company worked so hard to provide.

PDCA AUDITING

This book discusses the tools and methods required to be a great auditor or to teach auditors how to be great. While each chapter is dedicated to a particular concept, the universal application of PDCA makes possible a high degree of confidence, understanding, and control of the auditing function.

Chapters 2 and 3 explain the PDCA cycle as an auditor's best friend, a systematic and comprehensive approach to examining process plans and their implementation within your organization and how well they're doing. Chapter 4 visualizes the PDCA cycle as a complete process and explores the special place processes have in transforming plans into realities.

Chapter 5 examines how processes link together into a system, one of which is ISO 9001:2000. We will look at the standard as it was intended: a system designed to provide top management with the best information possible to make informed decisions. Chapter 6 examines section 4.1, the primary PDCA section of the standard, and its ability to create systemic improvement.

Chapter 7 introduces ISO section 7.1 and the PDCA Audit Master, a tool that anyone can use to audit a process, an objective, or even the quality policy itself.

Chapter 8 combines the PDCA Audit Master and the ISO 9001:2000 PDCA Guide used when auditing specific areas within the organization. The standard is explained in the language of PDCA, allowing even the novice auditor to perform a highly meaningful and in-depth audit.

Chapter 9 completes the process of providing value to top management and the entire organization through PDCA auditing and the process of corrective action and follow-up.

The appendixes complete the study of PDCA auditing. The Audit Master and the ISO 9001:2000 PDCA Guide appear in Appendixes A and B, respectively. Appendix C presents a previous audit of a PVC pipe manufacturing facility, including explanations and references to records.

SUMMARY

Good quality and good business begin with top managers making plans to avoid unacceptable risks. And the greatest risk to any company is to not know exactly what its customers want.

Planning is far more than the first step, however, because it sets in motion what will be the rest of the PDCA cycle. A good plan will be understood by everyone in the organization for what it can accomplish in the never-ending work of supplying more acceptable products to customers. A good plan needs less promoting, is easily understood, and gathers momentum quickly. And because it is the beginning, the *P* of the PDCA cycle, it has a special significance in establishing the process that follows.

Of course, the better the plan, the greater the likelihood of success. The next chapter is all about planning and the trail it both establishes and leaves behind. As auditors, our journey follows that trail throughout the organization, often moving from one department to the next, to decide for ourselves if it leads to better risk control and satisfied customers. We want to take that information back to the top mangers who approved the original plan and tell them what we learned along the way. Our work will possibly help them decide whether money invested in the plan was well spent or if more money is required to reach the intended outcome. As a result of following that trail, our audits become powerful tools for top management decisions, generating improvement to the planning process and ultimately the success of the company.

2

Plan, Do: The Beginning of the PDCA Cycle

Where would the quality profession be without acronyms? In the 1930s, Walter Shewhart is credited with the creation of a process improvement model called the *PDCA cycle,* or PDCA. The acronym stands for *Plan, Do, Check,* and *Act.* Of course, planning has always been of primary importance to achieving a desired outcome. But with the addition of doing what was planned, checking on its ability to do what was intended, and then acting on that information to make improvements, the initial plan is made complete. A complete plan is more than a good idea. In fact, the difference between a great plan and a wonderful idea is execution. After all, "Faith without deeds is no faith at all."

It's common sense that all organizations must effectively manage their people and finances to accomplish their plans. The ultimate responsibility to look after the company's resources falls on top management, whose first job is to avoid waste and unnecessary risks. Having only resources such as money and people to manage, they need lots of good information to best decide where to apply them. And the best application of resources shelters the company or service from threats to its survival.

So, what's the worst thing that could happen? In one way or another, I've asked that question many times of top managers, and the answer is always more revealing than if I'd asked "How's business?" Invariably, their answers about the worst thing that could happen to themselves or their business dredge up one or more serious threats from competitors, a vital program they fear will not succeed, or a problem they've tried to solve for a long time but which just gets worse. Each is a threat to current or future success, and of course that threat grows larger when nothing is done about it.

PLAN

Plans are created to respond to ideas, hopes, beliefs, desires, fears, and a host of other subjective thoughts and concerns. And even plans based on objective facts, such as regulatory compliance components or machinery capabilities, are not immune to emotionally driven, subjective thinking. The point is that even the most careful business judgment is laced with the personal beliefs of those who made the evaluation.

For that reason, planning requires data instead of hunches. Data are objective facts, although some would argue that their objectivity is often diminished as they're subjected to analysis and interpretation. But a reliance on good data as the basis for determining the degree of risk is still the best insurance against a plan that's driven instead by personalities and guesswork. A company that says it knows what its customers want should be able to supply objective evidence to that claim. The same is true for market weaknesses and threats. An objective approach will utilize trade journals, direct sales experience with customers, survey results, service records, complaints, competitors' profiles, and a great many other potential sources. The importance of a complete and accurate assessment of the threat must not be overlooked in the rush to formulate a plan to manage it. And haste that creates a flawed or wasteful plan can be more damaging than the unchecked consequences of the original threat.

Auditors are in a unique position to see the strength of any plan by taking a measure of its ability to do what it was designed to do: control a specific threat or unacceptable risk. That's why a comprehensive PDCA audit begins with a very simple but all-important question that essentially asks: What would be the risk to the organization if your work, or the work in this department, were not successful? Asking this question exposes the threat or risk that the process being audited is designed to control. And from this point onward, the audit becomes little more than following a path through the methods and the ultimate results of those controls.

And so, armed with objective information, the work of preparing the plan begins. Most rely on a team of managers and other experts to sort through what is known about the situation in order to best uncover the actions that will most likely remedy the current state of affairs. Sounds simple, but formulating the best plan, a complete plan, requires far more than deciding what action to take.

Steven Covey describes one of his *7 Habits of Highly Effective People* as the ability to "Begin with the End in Mind." A life plan or a business plan—it makes no difference, because without the ability to imagine the outcome, a plan by either an individual or an entire organization lacks the ability to focus on what's really important. Without a future vision, a point that is understood as the moment when something requiring effort is achieved, the chances of success are limited.

Here's an example. To many in the United States, the constant battle of weight control is a very real part of their lives. Dieting and the products that support weight loss have become a multimillion-dollar business, yet the overall success of many diet plans is highly questionable. People begin a diet with firm resolve and determination, yet either abandon it before they see results, or lose weight only to gain it all back again. Over and over, the pattern of partial success is repeated until dieters either accept their condition or decide to enlist medical help. Then why do most diets fail, given that a clear vision of the final result should be easy to imagine?

They fail because the vision is only partial. Few can initially imagine, let alone accept, that the real outcome of a successful diet is a complete change of lifestyle. Not only eating habits, but also exercise and health choices are actually involved. Dieting as willpower and daily scale watching is fine for weight reduction but does not prepare the dieter for an enjoyable life as a thinner, happier, healthier, and more energized person.

The same can be said for an organization that decides it must become lean and aggressive because of bureaucratic and sluggish practices that have become commonplace and that threaten its ability to compete. The vision that's required to achieve a lean posture is not one of belt tightening, slashed budgets, eventual layoffs, and additional stress and tension. It's unfortunate that too often this is what most believe to be the "hard truth" necessary to reach their goal. Instead, the organization should imagine a stimulating, energized, customer-intimate, creative, and operationally efficient culture. The rest will fall in place naturally as the new culture emerges. Each approach, whether focusing on cutting costs or creating a new culture, requires entirely different plans. The imagined outcome, or what Covey calls the "first creation," is an essential component of developing a plan. But the choice of images is entirely up to senior management to develop and promote.

A plan with a vision creates several other natural opportunities. If we know where we're going, it's possible to measure how much time we've spent and how far we have to go in order to reach specific milestones along the way. Suddenly, then, planning moves from an abstract vision to several very real steps that will indicate whether the plan is proceeding as expected. The result is a plan with teeth and substance, capable of measurement along the way to determine its success.

Because a plan is the starting point of any project, it actually defines the same things that are obvious to anyone who has ever run a race. Imagine the starting line of a relay race. To begin with, everyone starts by facing the same direction. Is it conceivable that the runners would be milling around, looking at the stands and their fellow runners, until the gun is fired to begin the race? Obviously, that behavior would be expected as they arrive and prepare. But then prior to the actual run they take their places, set their feet, and concentrate on the ground directly ahead. Looking forward, muscles tensed and body set, each is thinking exactly the same thing: Follow the plan, win the race. As auditors, we want not only to learn what top management's plan is, but also to detect an awareness and use of the plan that unites the members of the organization. What unites them in the same manner as that group of runners on the starting line, each ready to go, facing the same direction, and following a plan to succeed?

Called *culture,* the energy within an organization is much like those runners at the starting line and during the race that follows. A well-designed and well-communicated plan will make sense to everyone and inspire them to begin each day facing the same direction and working to reach the finish line. The team spirit will be easy to recognize, the common bond between players will be evident, and the language will often be similar from one department to the next. They're all "on the same page." Their energy is flowing in the same direction, working to stimulate each other's efforts in order to achieve the results promised by the plan. And as such, they contribute to each other's success for their mutual benefit. Auditors are in a perfect place to discover if the plan really has the support of the workers within the system. They can visit any section of the operation to follow up on each phase of the plan and determine if one person or department is handing off the baton as planned or if there are several separate races under way that conflict with each other. This takes patience and practice, but the tools we'll be discussing in later chapters will help to bring this issue to the surface.

DO

Using the same relay race metaphor, think about that moment when the gun actually fires. If a camera were to take a picture of that instant, what would you see? Smoke is visible from the barrel of the gun and most are still at the starting blocks with muscles just beginning to push their legs forward on to the track ahead. Now advance forward a bit to the point where everyone is actually running, and notice that the pack remains much as it was at the starting line. Early in the race, everyone has essentially the same progress, direction, speed, and desire. Now fast-forward to the race's conclusion and take a look at the same group of runners. What do you see? Perhaps one or two are struggling to finish first, neck-and-neck and running hard. The rest are either well back or have dropped out for one reason or another.

What happened to them? Why are only one or two runners typically leading the pack instead of the same bunched field that lined up at the starting line? Aside from individual differences—and while many would argue that those differences are the basis of one's success over another—the reason one wins in a balanced field is either a better plan or better execution. They *do* it better than the competition. They run according to a plan that was decided long before the starting gun, and they execute that plan faithfully.

Let's examine this closely from a quality perspective. Using a stopwatch, runner A is timed during practice. Her timing is recorded for five practice heats and an average determined. Research of the competing runners' times indicates that her average is sufficient to beat each of her competitors. Her race plan involves a final sprint in the last lap.

It's now race day and she's the favorite for obvious reasons. The gun sounds and the runners leave the blocks. But because she's confident of her ability to win, she decides to change the plan and sprint first to enlarge her lead from the pack and win with an even greater margin of distance between herself and the others. You probably know the rest of the story. Her loss was not driven simply by a misplaced confidence in her abilities, but rather *she changed the plan.* All previous measurements of her ability were developed according to a defined plan, one she disregarded, and thus she found that her performance stalled at the final lap. She'd run out of steam early, and the result was a loss of focus and performance.

The plan and its implementation are linked. Change the plan and everything else changes. Change how the plan is executed or disregard the plan entirely and you can expect the same result as navigating a rudderless boat. The point is clear: Plan and Do are different sides of the same coin. Done well, a good plan is a winner.

As auditors, we should be careful and persistent in comparing the plan with what's actually going on in the organization. After all, developing the plan costs money and it was expected to be done very carefully, according to preapproved activities. When those activities are not followed, the costs are different and can easily spin out of control—just as for a runner who decides to run a different race from what was previously planned. What was planned must be done so that progress can be checked against the plan. Success or failure of the project is the result of careful and controlled action to accomplish what's intended. Auditors are given the opportunity to investigate and report to top management on how the plan is being done, and hopefully to create a path to greater understanding of the plan's success.

3

Check, Act and the Process Model: Completing the Cycle

In the preceding chapter we explored the planning and doing phases of the PDCA cycle. The journey has begun—the first step has been taken. Hopefully, the organization has decided on a customer-driven plan to avoid any known risks, and the work is now underway within the organization. Top management, basing their decisions on factual information, approved the plan and expectations are upbeat and positive. So, after the plan is devised and implemented, what comes next? Does the implementation of new or improved processes simply continue with confidence that all will proceed as planned, or is there more to consider?

CHECK

The internal audit process is an examination of how well the plan is carried out. It therefore comprises the next phase of the PDCA model: a check of the processes themselves. Much of the audit process is actually detective work, and the best detectives look first for motive. In process driven auditing, motive is pretty simple: If the process in question is not done well, there are going to be lots of problems within the system. So the motivation to perform is driven by the risk of what might happen as a consequence of poor performance.

The auditor is not only given the task of checking whether the process is working according to plan, but also must determine if the risk it was designed to control has been effectively managed. This two-level examination is required if audit results are to be meaningful to top management, who must determine how and where best to spend the company's money. An audit that only investigates whether a process is working according to plan, but doesn't then search out whether that plan took care of the risk it was designed to control, is only half complete and of questionable value to top management. They need to know more than what's on the surface to make their decisions. And a well-run process that makes things no one wants is management's worst nightmare. (The old saying that summarizes this condition is "throwing good money after bad.") Good audits check processes for what they were designed to do, and then go further to tell top management if they spent their money wisely by checking the effectiveness of the process within the system.

In most organizations, either good, exceptional, or suboptimal performance is noticed. Immediately or over a period of time, everyone usually recognizes the best working parts of any operation, and their methods are often adopted elsewhere to improve. The same holds true in those areas of every organization that just can't seem to keep up. They are recognized as underachievers, are often given special considerations, and tend to force other departments and functions to work at their tempo, regardless of market demands.

The *theory of constraints* describes this situation as common to every system, one in which the weakest link defines the strength of the entire chain. And rather than going into the particulars of this engaging and basic theory, the fundamental truth of constraints thinking is one for every auditor to recognize: Even in the strongest of systems, there always is a weakest link. Furthermore, within each process is a series of actions, one of which is weaker than the others. Effective auditors are looking for the weakest link, the one area that tends to dictate to all others, in order to help the operation see itself in a way that can lead to improvement.

But the search for the weakest link has its place. And as the auditor works through the details within the process, he or she is looking for weaknesses in compliance—compliance, that is, to the process as originally planned. So, if the process defines performance as, for example, completion of a particular form in 36 hours, and available evidence proves that the form actually moved through the department well within that time frame, there is no process weakness. Performance is well within the planned parameters.

But if there is a need elsewhere for that form in 8 hours, the weakness is in the connection to the next link, which hasn't effectively communicated to the process owners to speed things up. So, system weaknesses are caused by both process-specific issues such as a failure to operate as planned and systems-level issues such as a lack of critical communication between processes. The actual weak link is often operating at more than one level within a system. For that reason, auditors must often look deeper than the first discovery whenever an apparent problem is detected.

Think of the iceberg model. At the surface, there is a process problem that everyone recognizes simply because it's visible. To use the 36-hour paperwork processing time as an example, the department that's doing the work isn't actually in trouble on the surface. They're doing their work according to the plan. But underneath the surface, the lack of connection to the people who actually use the form they produce indicates a real and potentially risky weak link. Add the potential for other problems with the next operation in line, right down to the ultimate customer, and one delay can cascade into an even greater systems-level weakness. That's potentially a very large set of issues, all of which are reversible through what looks like a surface-level process improvement to speed up the paperwork by revising the plan.

Issues like these are deceptive because below the surface may also be the real reason why this link between one department's needs and another appears to be so weak. Do the people in each department get along well, or is there considerable tension between them? Was the process designed so long ago that it simply became obsolete under new, more demanding business requirements? Is the same detachment between departments apparent in not only this audit, but others as well?

These probing, carefully stated questions and observations are the hallmark of a good auditor and often require considerable experience to master. New auditors must therefore beware of assuming that the first answer is the best answer. Most often, there are a series of underlying reasons for poor performance, many of which lie below the immediate and visible problem.

Checking that the plan worked as designed is *compliance auditing.* Checking that the plan not only worked as designed but also delivered an excellent product is *process auditing.* In order to audit a process, there needs to be a check of all the classic components of input, transformation, resources, controls, and output, as shown in Figure 3.1. They are the primary components of an often exciting series of discoveries.

A process has an input, loosely defined as anything that must be transformed into an output. Examples include checks from customers, perhaps processed by the office manager and mailed to the bank along with a deposit slip. Along the way, the office manager used certain resources to accomplish her work, such as the stamp and envelope she finally dropped into the mailbox. Controls involved to process the checks included the required bank deposit slip, completed exactly the way the bank so carefully explained to her the last time she forgot to add the checks properly.

Together, the input, transformation, resources, controls, and output created a flow of controlled, measurable activity. The office manager may not think of her work as a process, but if looked at from high above, her actions appear to be identical from one day to the next. Each day, a more or less steady number of checks are processed in a relatively similar amount of time. If she often makes mistakes in her work, an average error rate can be determined and a process refinement added to reduce them. For instance, perhaps the bank needs the deposit by a certain time in the day and she is always rushed to meet the deadline. Once again, a process improvement

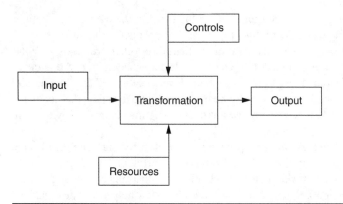

Figure 3.1   Process diagram.

may be added if the average time per check is determined and a suitable amount of time allotted to do the work based on the number of checks received by a predetermined time in the day. The point is that any process carries a possible means of measurement—whether it is processing time, defect rate, quantity per hour, or a percentage of overall efficiency.

The plan was supposed to have already determined these measurement points. Auditors must first ask what those measurements are and then be shown evidence of how things are working. If the plan was to decrease patient wait time by 50 percent over 6 months, and the audit takes place during the third month of the program, the expected reduction should be at or near 25 percent. If, instead, the situation is unchanged, the auditor is faced with having to ask a series of questions to determine if the program is bogged down or if some other component is not yet in place for an acceptable reason. Either way, the planned measurement system must be in place and the results recorded in the audit report.

Most companies do a great job of doing what they believe is right. Some plan more than others before they rush into doing things, but few do as well in checking to see if all their activities are really working as planned.

"It's obvious that things are going well—just look at our third quarter profits!" "If we were really missing the mark, we'd not have so many repeat orders, would we?" Both these statements may be true, but probably neither was determined to be a measurement point in any of the individual processes within a company's system of operations. Claims such as these are a strong indication that process measurements are not in place, but are justified instead by generalizations that often only serve to cover up areas in need of improvement. The auditor should be engaged in a search for *objective evidence* that processes are operating according to planned arrangements. Whenever and wherever an auditor cannot obtain such information, it's time to consider several options:

- Ask more probing questions. Often the data are buried within the operating system and simply not recognized by the person being audited. He or she is too close to the system and, for whatever reason, does not connect what is available with what you're requesting.

- Ask the next in line. Sometimes the recipient of the process under audit conducts measurements of its input. It just may be that the measurement you're searching for is in another department.

- Ask the audit subject why there are no measurements. This approach often produces surprising results. If there truly are none, ask how the department knows how it's doing, and especially how personnel know where or what to improve. For example, suppose a department store jewelry division waits on 30 people per hour. An average of 10 sales are made in the same time frame, which computes to a 33 percent sales rate. As a baseline measurement, the division can now develop a plan to improve the sales rate and measure its effectiveness each month.

ACT

It was previously stated that the internal audit process is an examination of how well the plan is carried out. If the audit subject is taking proper measurements of its process and indications are good or bad, excellent or inferior, the surprising fact is that *in either case* action should follow to improve the process. Let's look at conditions at both ends of the scale: excellent results and poor results.

Excellent results are the logical outcome of an excellent plan that was faithfully executed. Remember the runner who, had she followed the plan, was a shoo-in to win, but decided to change things at the last minute? Suppose that she actually did run the race according to all the training and planning that preceded the event and was the clear winner. In fact, due to the competitiveness of the race she also beat her previous best time. Would her trainer now decide to cut her practice time in half and devote more of his time to other runners, or would he work more closely with her to improve more subtle and complex aspects of her running style?

It's been said that "nobody wins like a winner," and there's a great deal of logic to that phrase. True winners are the ones who work at winning. They perfect a unique style that's best suited to their particular assets and that simultaneously minimizes their weaknesses. So the winners are winning by design and hard work—always a source of analysis (check) and revision of the plan (act), to make further refinements and keep on winning.

Poor results, on the other hand, are the logical outcome of:

- An excellent plan that was poorly executed

- A poor plan that was executed well

- A poor plan that was poorly executed

After the dust settles and the results are in (check), the poorly performing process has one of the above three choices to choose from to begin the work of trying again. But most important to the PDCA cycle is the realization that both good and poor results are treated in the same manner, as opportunities to learn and improve.

The act function in the PDCA cycle is what the organization or department does with the results of the measurements from the check function. One of the most important of ISO 9000's eight management principles is that decisions must be based on facts. And measurements are objective facts that management can act upon to further improve operations. As auditors we are looking for the measurements to have meaning to the audit subjects, as the raw material they use to improve the process.

"The world is drowning in data!" Since the introduction of computers and the Internet, a worldwide data explosion has occurred. The same is true in most companies and service organizations as their networks increasingly require more and more memory and features to keep up with system demands. The difference between having the data and actually doing meaningful things with the data has become the subject of widespread concern. Companies who act on their data, who use the information not only to monitor operations but also to point the way to improvement, are actively reinventing their processes to squeeze out the maximum efficiency possible.

As auditors, we are looking for that last phase of the PDCA cycle, the one in which a department analyzes its data and makes a decision to try something new. In doing so, the original plan is typically modified to redirect controls or resources. In fact, once a process plan is modified, it's really a new process with new things to do and check along the way. This is why the PDCA model is called a *cycle*. It cycles by spiraling upward from one level to another, each stronger then the last, each producing better results than the previous plan.

PDCA is an engine for improvement and a logical model to apply to the audit process. If the department or function of an operation develops and executes its process according to the PDCA model, there ought to be several common elements that the auditor can use to investigate the particular workings of the audit subject:

- What is the risk that the plan was designed to control?

- Who's responsible for the plan's proper execution?

- What is the actual plan?

- How's it going?

- Did the plan control the risk or not?

The answers to these questions form a report to top management that will be the subject of the remaining chapters of this book. Application of PDCA will include the introduction of the Audit Master, a tool designed for use in every audit to guide the auditor's questions, regardless of where or what he or she is auditing. Also included is the PDCA Guide, a cross-reference tool to pull sections of the ISO 9001:2000 Standard into the proper areas of the Audit Master. Together, these two tools enable a novice to immediately begin gaining experience as an internal auditor and provide valuable insight and reporting to top management. Because internal auditors are often drawn from the rank and file within the organization, they need all the help they can get. The next several chapters are designed to accomplish just that.

4

PDCA as a Process: Making the Most of a Good Plan

The complete PDCA cycle is also a process. In fact, the four PDCA elements—Plan, Do, Check, Act—are actually a series of events that easily translate into the process terminology introduced in the previous chapter: input, transformation, controls, resources, and output. As always, the entire chain of events begins with a plan.

Planning is the start of any process. Let's say you're about to go on a business trip to a remote place. The process you use to accomplish the goal of getting to the meeting begins with thinking and planning, which might involve sorting through a large amount of information. If it's tough to get the information you need, you may be faced with a much harder task than simply calling a travel agent or booking transportation on the Internet. When information is hard to get the planning stage has to account for it, and you have to make special arrangements, work harder, or practice patience. The same is true for any department in a company that relies on another department to provide raw materials, paperwork, or some other input to the process. Planning is an input function, the first element of every process, as shown in this diagram:

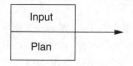

The process cannot begin without a good plan, or chaos will result. The *input,* the reason to begin, should be the product of careful thinking. After all, there's a real risk involved, as observed previously: A poor plan rarely produces excellent results. When the future of the new product line is at stake, the plan or input to everything that follows must be well designed, regardless of the obstacles.

The next PDCA element's relationship to those of a process is fairly straightforward. *Doing* is what happens after the plan is developed. Therefore, in process terms, doing is the same as *transformation,* as shown here:

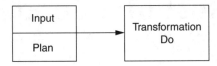

The work performed or the tasks completed are nothing more than the ultimate activities that are first imagined in the plan. If the work is done well and the plan is good, there should be a positive outcome. Something good will result from the "doing."

The finished product is described in process terms as the *output,* which PDCA calls the result or *act.*

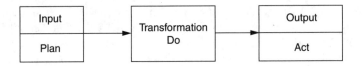

Of course, there's a very important PDCA element that's missing! The model we've been building could easily lead us into doing things that would be mindless at best, and at worst a disaster. Fortunately, a process also contains two other elements—controls and resources—and one of these holds the final PDCA element as well.

That final PDCA element is the *checking* function. A bit of thinking about the difference between process controls and resources pretty much narrows the choice: *Controls* are closest to something that ultimately has a hand in checking whether what is done is actually done properly. After all, if you add controls to a process, you've more or less forced the folks who do the work to always make sure they do things within those controls. And the best way to ensure that you're working within those controls is to check from time to time. Thus, we now have a complete diagram:

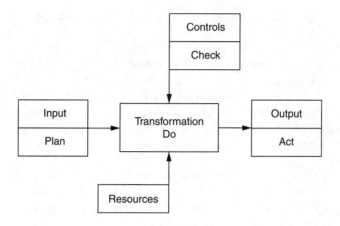

The best part of combining PDCA and process elements is the ability to understand what people do and how they do it in a new way. A process uses resources such as money, time, machinery, and labor to transform raw materials into a finished product. But without controls, the inability to contain costs could lead to real trouble. So, controls are a necessary and often welcome part of everything we do.

Remember the runner in Chapter 2, who at the last minute decided to run her race differently? She practiced a carefully designed race plan, one that took into account her resources of natural ability, strength, and endurance. Essentially, the race plan was nothing more than a control of those resources, and when she abandoned those controls the race was lost. There are numerous examples of wasted or uncontrolled resources, due simply to a lack of checking.

Most plans are designed to work. In fact, most begin when it's almost assured that they will. Too often, the logic of planned success clouds the judgment of those who would otherwise exercise the same care in checking as they do in planning. Leaders often neglect to check how a process is functioning simply because it's working. But the difference between a process that is working and one that is working to its highest ability cannot be decided without checking. And because each improvement to the original plan adds strength to the process that can only be measured against prior checks, it's essential that they be done frequently and results forwarded to decision makers.

To prove how easy it is to disregard the check function in the PDCA cycle, let's use an example that most are familiar with: Dan is concerned that his car's gas mileage is below what it once was and decides to get a tune-up and oil change. He figures that once the work is completed, his car will run like new and gas mileage will be at its best. The auto service center called Dan when the work was completed, and as he drove away it was clear that the car was performing very well. A smile crossed his face as he decided that regardless of the mileage, the improvements were worth the cost.

If the plan was to feel better while Dan drove his car, he succeeded. His PDCA cycle was complete when he patted the dashboard, smiled, and thought to himself that the auto service was money well spent. But the original plan was to improve gas mileage, not to simply feel better. The switch from one focus or desired outcome to another grew out of success. And while the plan all along may have been to better enjoy the ride, Dan omitted mileage checks both before and after the work was performed. No wonder the feeling of having done well to service the car became more important than the original plan of improved fuel economy.

Dan's methods are far from unusual. Service and industry organizations—both for-profit and not-for-profit—routinely succeed, and through that success often decide that the original checks are no longer necessary. And all this happens at the expense of whatever improvements could follow from investigating, testing, or otherwise following the PDCA cycle. Without the check function, the plan is only partially complete. And the result of an incomplete plan is often the illusion of success. Dan's car may drive well, feel more responsive, and have a new-car smell—but the hole in the gas tank is still there.

For the auditor, the check function of a process or plan is fertile territory for discovering wasteful practices. First of all, too many companies do not check performance of their key processes on a regular basis. And if they do, it's often the case that top management is unaware of the results. It's not uncommon to find that the PDCA cycle is abandoned when the plan apparently works.

"Why bother to check how it's doing—isn't it obvious that things are much better?" On a very superficial level, this may be absolutely true and performance might well be excellent. But without measurement, there's no ability to gauge effectiveness, let alone discover the exact nature of the new performance output and its use of resources. When checking is considered a bother, look carefully at what's really going on. The ISO standard requires processes to be "monitored for effectiveness," not assumed to be effective. The reason these checks are so important is because they provide a valuable tool to top management. Management's analysis of process and system effectiveness ultimately decides what resources will be applied in each area, so it's not to be left to chance or assumptions. Auditors should be especially careful to find and report process and systems inspections.

Auditors examine processes. The entire audit process is a checking function, a methodical (planned) examination of how a process controls its resources in the transformation of its inputs into outputs. Records are created in the process of doing both the work of the process itself and the audit of that work. The audit report is a record of the auditor's journey through the process he or she examined. Contained within the report is evidence of records found during the audit. These records serve as evidence that the planning, work, inspection, and completion of a process were witnessed during the audit.

Records are important because they represent something that was agreed to or something that happened in the past that was worthy of saving. When auditors examine processes, they are always looking for records that prove what they are being told by those they audit. As such, each record that confirms the truth of what they are examining serves as a reality check, a confirmation that what they are hearing is actually happening. Records are the most important check function of any audit, the objective evidence of what was done, how it was done, and whether the work was itself checked before it was delivered to the next in line.

Records of inspection results, customer surveys, and testing are evidence of checks performed during the process. Auditors are always on the lookout for these records to prove that the check function is well established within the process and that the results of those checks indicate that the plan is working as originally designed.

The process that controls its resources through PDCA is an *improvement engine.* By monitoring its work and output, a process is always alert to new possibilities and opportunities. Revisions are welcome because the information that flows through the operation is interesting and highly relevant. Each new discovery improves one part or another of the original plan, and the result is an upward spiral of ideas and actions, modifications and enhancements.

5

Integrating ISO 9001:2000: Systems and Their Processes

We've all heard of the person who has "a system for everything." Such people can be a challenge because of the often rigid manner in which they live their lives, but they can also teach us a valuable lesson. Functioning in such a way that assures success isn't all that bad an outlook, when to lose would end your chances of ever functioning again. Examples include the work of airplane pilots, surgeons, and refinery workers, and the tactics of military campaigns. Quite a few things in life are important enough to develop a system in order to succeed.

Systems are nothing more than a chain of processes designed to accomplish a specific task. We rely on systems to drive, cook meals, apply makeup, get married, and even to read these words. In one way or another, processes are linked together, enabling an infinite number of systems to take place. And they do! Even when we're not aware of them, processes link the activities of our days and nights, providing clarity and direction to our lives. Let's look at a typical day to understand how powerfully processes and systems define our activities.

The alarm rings at exactly 6 A.M. to wake you from a night's sleep. You set it last evening in order to allow yourself enough time to get ready for work at 8. When you shut off the alarm, you're ending a process begun the previous night. Now it's off to the bathroom for a shower and all the other things you normally do prior to making breakfast. When you enter the kitchen to make coffee, you're ending the process that cleaned your face and body in preparation for the upcoming workday. Breakfast over, you take a second cup of coffee back to the bathroom as you brush your teeth, comb your hair, and make a final attempt to look your best before getting dressed for the day.

Once again, each activity is a process, completed in a specific order, one linked to the next to accomplish a single objective—your personal system of getting to work.

Processes are linked activities within a system. As we've learned, processes are transformations of inputs into outputs. In a system, one process's output becomes the next process's input. The processes are connected in much the same manner as links on a chain are connected. Even links at the farthest extremes of the chain share equal dependence with each other when force is applied. And if the chain were to break, all the links share the consequences. In other words, the system fails when just one link breaks.

Shipments are delayed when machines break down unexpectedly. Production slows or stops when raw materials are late or substandard. Hospital waiting rooms become overcrowded when poor planning results in a shortage of doctors or other specialists. Congratulations if you're thinking that risk was not properly managed in each instance, but be aware that systems are often not designed to operate under all potential threats. The best planning tries to predict as many threats as possible, but the complexity of a system can make this task extremely difficult—that is, unless a model is available to serve as a guide or checklist of best practices.

That's what the ISO 9001:2000 Standard tries to accomplish. Its function is that of a master plan for avoiding risk and managing threats to an organization. And it, too, uses PDCA as its primary operating model.

Section 4.1 of ISO 9001:2000 is often called the "heart and soul" of the standard because each part of this element is ultimately repeated many times throughout the rest of the document. It calls for top management to first decide what processes are required for the organization to function properly. Once that's accomplished, management is asked to demonstrate how these processes are linked and work together—in other words, to explain the system and where each process fits within it. A series of other considerations follow, such as determining measurements for each process (in order to check on their success within the system), acknowledging the obvious need to make money, identifying the people and time available to get the work done, reviewing things on a regular basis, and finally acting on information received through those reviews. Now if you've read that last sentence carefully, you've noticed that each of these considerations sounds awfully familiar. For instance:

1. Management is asked to explain the system and how it works. That's nothing more than asking for the plan.

2. Making sure that the people, money, and time are available is just another way of saying that resources are required to do the plan.

3. What are the measurements used for? To check on how the plan is doing.

4. And finally, reviewing things in order to act on that information is the act stage of the PDCA cycle.

Throughout the ISO 9001:2000 Standard, the same pattern emerges over and over. And for good reason! Each element—such as purchasing, human resources, or design and production (called "Product Realization" in the standard)—is actually a process in itself. We've already learned that processes use the PDCA cycle to transform their inputs into outputs, and so it's no surprise that within each ISO element is the chance to see PDCA in action.

Getting ready for work is a process that involved all the PDCA steps. Shutting off the alarm ended the plan for phase one: getting out of bed. If you'd set the alarm too late, you'd act differently based on checking the time as you turned off the alarm. And all along the way, similar checks and the resulting actions happen normally to obtain and use information in order to succeed.

The authors of the ISO 9001:2000 Standard understood the power of this simple concept and designed most of the elements using PDCA either directly or indirectly. As such, it's a system designed to provide top management with the best information possible to make informed decisions. And that's true because PDCA can be applied to any activity within an organization and is designed to produce improvement regardless of the success level of that activity.

In the preceding chapter, processes that were managed using PDCA were called *improvement engines*. This was not a casual comment. When PDCA is understood as an ally to the art of managing a process, its true strength comes to the surface. And when PDCA is fully in effect, auditors can easily observe the telltale signs. First and foremost, things are improving. Regardless of whether the plan succeeds or fails, PDCA cycles result in a new and improved approach. Departments or entire organizations that practice PDCA are often very upbeat and positive places to visit. They've learned that PDCA is a tool that allows them to discover new things, even when they make mistakes—and the result is an operation that is involved, always eager to learn how their plans are developing, and uses their best analysis to make corrections to their plans. Positive energy and a sense of pride are not uncommon in these organizations, and auditors often find themselves fortunately swept up by the enthusiasm of the people they interview.

Another sign of PDCA is *accountability*. When the opportunity to improve the original plan is always available, most people welcome the process of making meaningful checks of their work. And the better their information, the more potential they have to succeed. PDCA is win-win and accountability thrives in that environment.

There is also a high level of communication in a PDCA culture. Auditors will find people who are used to talking to each other, often quite candid and open about their system's performance, and eager to describe things in detail. There are meetings and discussions about performance, customers, pricing, competition, materials, and new market trends throughout the organization, not just in Sales and Marketing. As much as possible, everyone's working to stay on the same page because their success depends on maintaining a high degree of concentration to stick to the current plan. Because of the many careful checks and subtle revisions to the plan that often follow, communication in a PDCA culture is as important as profits. Auditors will often find multiple, often very creative, methods for getting the latest information to everyone in the department or organization, so that everybody knows the latest score and the most recent revision of the plan.

Improvement, accountability, pride, and strong communication are traits that any organization wants and any auditor can easily recognize during the audit. Top management will be involved as they participate in the action and encourage the flow of information and the development of the people within the company. This is the intent of ISO 9001:2000—to create a system of continually improving processes within a system. PDCA is the engine of improvement for each of these linked processes as well as for the entire system of processes that make up the organization. PDCA is therefore working at two levels simultaneously within a company: at a simple level within each process, and at the more complex systems level where the output of one process becomes the input to the next.

For example, a juggler is able to throw three or more balls into the air and somehow keep them all in motion in a steady circle in front of him. The juggler is managing a complex system requiring balance, concentration, exact timing, and skill. He is constantly checking the condition of each ball, its speed and arc, its rate of spin, and its weight, as well as the combined locations of all the balls in relation to each hand. Talk about real-time PDCA! The plan is constantly changing in small but very critical ways, based on how his juggling system is operating at any one time. One ball in the wrong place changes everything. The need to act must be communicated quickly enough to maintain the system—to skillfully keep all the balls in the air.

There are two sections of the ISO 9001:2000 Standard that, working together, explain how to go about juggling the processes and how to keep them in motion to create steady improvement in the system. It is here that we begin the practice of auditing, because we need to know the answers to two critical questions: What are the processes themselves? And, how is each process contributing to the common goal? The two ISO 9001:2000 sections are numbered 4.1 and 7.1, and we'll examine them in the next two chapters. Together, they form the building blocks, the primary components for use in developing a basic process auditing approach. Placing pieces of these two sections into four phases of each audit (Plan, Do, Check, Act) creates a powerful and amazingly easy-to-follow auditing process.

6

ISO 9001:2000 Section 4.1 and PDCA: The Big Picture

Section 4.1 ("General Requirements") is the beginning of the ISO 9001:2000 Standard, the first series of requirements that top management must adopt and apply to the organization. There are six elements: 4.1(a), 4.1(b), 4.1(c), and so forth. Although we mentioned these elements in the preceding chapter, a bit more detail will be valuable for reasons that will hopefully become clear as this story unfolds.

Sections 4.1(a) and 4.1(b) require top management to define the individual processes in the company's system, the sequence from one to the next, and the relationship between them. They could've simply asked, "What's the plan?" or the series of processes that top management believes must be in place to do the work of the organization. But what really is the work of the organization? What are all these processes ultimately designed to do, other than the obvious requirement to meet and exceed the customer's requirements?

It may seem obvious, but at the foundation of each process, at the place where it really matters, they all have to work! In other words, each process is a link, and there is a tremendous risk if any of them underperforms. Section 4.1 begins by asking top management not just what is going on in the company, but also what are the processes that must work well to manage the day-to-day risks of doing business. Why pay for a process that doesn't take care of something, that doesn't create value for the company and its customers? When ISO asks about processes and their relationship to each other, it's really asking top management to define what they believe they must do to effectively manage risk on a regular basis.

And so as auditors we begin the investigation of everything in the company by asking the people we meet what they believe is the risk that the process they work within is designed to manage. Simply, we begin by asking them to explain the consequences of not doing their work: What would happen? Where would things go wrong? Who would be affected, and what might be the worst thing that could happen? There will be more than a few who will tell you they've never been asked that question before, and that's really an amazing admission when you think about it. After all, we all work hard each day to meet deadlines, quotas, projections, and any number of requirements, but we almost never step back from all the activity and ask ourselves if the entire process is really doing all the things it should, let alone why it's so important to do what we do.

Top management decided, according to 4.1(a) and 4.1(b), that several important processes were necessary to carry out daily business. Okay, as auditors, we begin our work by going into each of those processes and asking what's so important. We do this because at the end of the day we want to know if each process actually performed as expected. And there's no better way to do that than to ask why something is important and investigate from there, through the four stages of PDCA, to find out if the risks have been identified and if the following issues have been addressed:

- Has a plan been developed to manage these risks?

- What work was or is being done according to that plan?

- What checks of that work are made against the original plan?

- What actions resulted, based on those checks, to improve managing the risks?

If the result of all this effort shows that the process is always improving, learning from its performance, and doing things as planned, the possible risks it was designed to manage should be under control as well. Of course, there are other specifics that lie within each section of the PDCA cycle. The next one just happens to be 4.1(c).

It stands to reason that once you know what the important processes are and how they all work together, it would be wise to have a basic idea of what is expected from them. And the best way to effectively operate and control these processes is to determine what you expect them to do and the measurements that can best be used to monitor their performance. Let's take a minute and go back to the auto tune-up example to explain why measurements and criteria are so important to developing any system of processes.

You may remember the plan to improve gas mileage from Chapter 4. In that story the owner wanted better mileage and decided to get a tune-up. What he didn't do was to think carefully about the expected improvement compared to the estimated price of service to his car. If, for example, the repair bill were more than $500, would the improved mileage over a year's time justify the cost if he only drives 8000 miles? Doing the math and finding out if the tune-up is worth the investment first requires deciding what facts, tolerances, and limits are important. Step one, therefore, is to determine these criteria. *Criteria* are the details, the facts and figures that people need to make good decisions. Once you've determined the criteria, you can take measurements against them.

Need to buy a new car after realizing that a tune-up will never really help? What are your criteria? Suppose that you have 2-year-old twins as well as a teenage daughter who's into soccer, and you work part-time as a football coach. Chances are, all these criteria are telling you to buy a mini-van or SUV. And if you do, at some point you may decide that your new van is working well based on your personal observations (measurements) and those of your family. Those observations are made in relation to your initial set of criteria. Do the van's two rear built-in child seats and extra room satisfy the important criteria of child safety and an active soccer schedule? Is there ample room for football equipment on game day? If the answer is yes to all, congratulations! The measurement against these criteria confirms that you've invested in the right vehicle for your family.

Whether in business or service organizations, each department is connected to the other directly or indirectly and often relies on the other for materials or information to do its job. Newspaper companies require details to work their way through the system quickly, one department after the other rushing information along as quickly as they can to meet a deadline. But while speed is a significant criterion in the newspaper business, it's far less important to farming and needlework. Those activities judge their success using criteria that let them take their time, allowing for all sorts of setbacks and adjustments along the way. Setting up a system of processes carries a responsibility to define measurement criteria for the entire system as well as for each process within it. Without measurement criteria the organization is flying blind, accepting any outcome as the best it could do "under the circumstances." Unfortunately, that excuse is often too little and too late.

And speaking of poor planning, what use are criteria and lots of great processes without the people, plant, time, and money to do their jobs? It's not enough to identify what's important and establish criteria—top management also has to put money there, too. It makes no sense to identify the important processes that will control risk and then not provide the people, time, equipment, and necessary training to make it work. And yet, amazingly, it happens all the time! That's why 4.1(d) calls for top management to provide the necessary resources for the system to work effectively. It's something top management must do. Remember, *resources* is a management term that includes everything requiring time and money.

Imagine that top management identified all the processes required to operate a hospital, but routinely angered patients by having fewer than the correct number of admitting nurses. Lines grow longer, tension is at the breaking point, people are shouting and crying, and still the situation repeats itself the next day and the next. Perhaps a manufacturing company expands its capacity by buying a new machine, but does not realize that the staff will require extensive training to operate it properly. Orders are accepted prior to receipt of the machine, installation day arrives, and suddenly the staff is expected to perform at an unreasonable level of quality and output.

ISO 9001:2000 recognizes that it takes both organization and adequate funding to make a system work effectively, and that's why it's important that auditors ask questions about these two components. Throughout the PDCA audit process we're asking people what tools they use for the work they do and, most importantly, whether they find that those tools are working well for them. There are countless examples of computer software, conveyer systems, forklifts, paint sprayers, answering systems, and other man-made contraptions that are underperforming and holding back the potential of people who feel forced to accept less than what they were expecting. In other words, what should've been a resource is instead a problem. Auditors are watchdogs for 4.1(d) and thereby are in a position to help top management understand where they need to apply new or better resources in the system of processes they're responsible for managing.

As a student of PDCA and processes, you're in familiar territory. Do you remember that the transformation of an input into an output requires both controls and (you guessed it!) resources? Perhaps now it's even more obvious how PDCA and processes are always working together as a team to create clarity and focus. ISO uses the process design and PDCA in combination as it walks top management through the six elements of section 4.1.

Element 4.1(d) requires top management to monitor effectiveness once the system is implemented. Implement is a *do* word, isn't it? And it couldn't be more clearly stated as section 4.1 moves from planning to doing: 4.1(a), 4.1(b), and 4.1(c) are planning elements. So here in 4.1(d) we've already defined the plan, decided how to measure it, and determined what sort of money it will take to do things accordingly. It's time to actually get busy and get to work! But the standard won't let us forget to monitor how well things are going as the work progresses. Actually, this reminder is an important part of 4.1(d), because without it the rest of the six elements in 4.1 would break down. Monitoring the process provides top management (and hopefully the rest of the company) with data and information that's vital to deciding whether the process and the system as a whole are working effectively in real time. And as for the PDCA cheerleaders in the crowd, they are already smiling because they know that without this information the next phase of PDCA wouldn't be possible.

You guessed it: A call to check is coming next. That's what 4.1(e) is all about. And much as the previous element didn't mince words about what was required, 4.1(e) is also direct and easy to understand:

4.1(e) – The organization shall monitor, measure, and analyze these processes.

The ISO 9001:2000 Standard is a PDCA system. Here in 4.1(e) there's absolutely no doubt that measuring the global system and its individual processes is a requirement, and as auditors we naturally serve a measurement function. We collect information about processes and their effect on the system, and then bring our conclusions to top management to help them make better decisions.

The same is true for a few other important elements in the standard, and it's not just a coincidence that they carry the requirement that they be documented. Nonconformance (especially customer complaints), corrective action, and auditing supply top management with solid information about how the organization is functioning, and together these elements serve as a check of the system's ability to supply good products and continue to improve. And to add strength to our audits, we actually use nonconformance and corrective action information along with previous audit findings to help us plan and develop our audit questions.

We develop or plan the audit's questions beforehand, to study and include as much information as necessary to do a thorough job of checking. When the audit is concluded we write a report about what we found, and as a final act we send that report to top management for review. Our report is a summary of what we were sent to check. And because of the importance of 4.1(e)—requiring that an organization monitor its processes—the auditor shares center stage with other processes within the system to accomplish this important assignment. Simply stated, as auditors our job is to monitor the organization's system of processes. We are, therefore, official agents of 4.1(e), hopefully acting on the authority of top management as their eyes and ears deep within the operation of the organization.

Once we've supplied our information, a certain amount of analysis is to be expected. Will the customer's reaction be positive if change occurs? Can the organization afford an indicated improvement to the plan, or will it have to limp along until the money is available? Are people disconnected from each other and the organization's objectives? And if something changes in one place within the system, what effect will that have on other processes?

But all the analysis is meaningless if nothing is done about the situation. That's where the last element of 4.1 and PDCA combine to make the necessary changes to the system. It's time to act. And once again, the standard is clearly written:

> 4.1(f) – The organization shall implement actions necessary to achieve planned results and continual improvement of these processes.

Acting on the information obtained from audits, nonconformance, directly from customers, and through all the internal systems within the organization is what top management is paid to do. They transform all the information they receive into new plans or into revisions of the original plan. Their leadership depends on the quality of all this input and on the hard choices they often must make for the greater good of the organization and their customers. At the end of the day, someone has to act on all the data and information to make a positive change—and as auditors we help others by supplying solid, factual information for those actions.

In world-class organizations, the plan is revised, perhaps resources are shifted to other areas, training may begin, or any number of new programs may be developed for improvement. There's a new beginning, a fresh start, even if it's simply to continue working within a strong and productive process. The end becomes the beginning as the act brings us to an improved plan. The circle is complete, and as auditors we were a key component in making it happen. We took 4.1(a) through 4.1(f) along with us as a guide, and in the process we walked through all the elements of the PDCA cycle. This is what we will do in each audit: We'll take section 4.1, and its lesser twin 7.1 ("Planning of Product Realization"), along with us to keep our focus and to make sure that wherever we audit, our journey will step through the full PDCA cycle on several levels simultaneously. The next chapter introduces the primary concepts that inspire the first of two tools we will use to accomplish this elevated goal.

7

Imagining an ISO 9001:2000 PDCA Audit: What Questions Would We Ask?

A mong other considerations, a well-planned trip relies on the accuracy and detail of a good map. Maps show the traveler much more than a graphic representation of the start and end points of a journey. Studying a map is a journey in itself—a journey of the mind where the traveler imagines what she might see and do along the way. An auditor's journey is no different. We are used to planning our audits carefully, in the process making both mental and often physical maps of our intended route to accomplish our work.

If, for example, you were asked to audit the Purchasing department of your organization it would be natural for you to imagine speaking to several people and visiting a minimum of two or three locations within your company. During the audit planning phase, you normally write down these particulars along with other information that might be of interest to you, such as prior nonconformance, problems from previous audits, and specific elements of the standard that are required to be in place. A comprehensive audit demands this level of research, but it also helps you, the informed auditor, to appreciate the terrain and past concerns that were important or had a significant effect on the people and places you will soon visit.

This planning stage is often called a *bench audit,* and in the process you're building a type of map as one thing leads naturally to the next. Getting from one issue to another begins to take shape as you imagine how to address each concern and where you will probably need to go to find the answers you seek.

Unfortunately, study of the ISO 9001:2000 Standard doesn't readily provide a complete PDCA map in regard to any one section. Besides, we've learned that the plan, do, check, and act functions of the standard are implied more than stated. And since they also exist on both a global (4.1) and a local (7.1) level, creating a good PDCA audit map would require an auditor who is an expert in understanding how and when to be thinking in generalities, or specifics—or both!

Sounds like a tough assignment, doesn't it? To get at the foundation of what's to come, let's imagine a PDCA Purchasing audit without any concern for the requirements listed in the Purchasing section (7.4) of the ISO 9001:2000 Standard. This time we're just interested in asking about planning, doing, checking, and acting on the information those checks provided.

So here's the scenario: Imagine that we both work at the same company, you're manager of the Purchasing department, and I walk into your office to conduct an internal audit. I'd introduce myself, and after several minutes of small talk I'd casually ask you a very simple question: "What would be the risk to the company if the purchasing process didn't work as planned?" In other words, I'm asking what would be the risk to the company if you or your staff weren't doing the work well.

The start of this journey is always the same: In order for there to be a plan, there must be a reason to plan. That's why I first asked you not what you do, but what probably would happen if you didn't do it. I want you to tell me what risks you are managing through your work—risks that are important enough to bring together you, your staff, and all the equipment, files, and furniture it takes to keep those risks under control. Remember, they're all resources, aren't they?

You tell me three things you believe are the primary risks the Purchasing department faces: (1) spending too much for the things the company buys, (2) ordering the wrong things and thereby slowing or stopping production, and (3) keeping the company's credit rating intact through the system your department's developed.

Now that I've written these down, I look back at you and ask how these three concerns are related to our company's goals and to our customers. I'm trying to connect the work that the Purchasing department does to the core mission of our company and to the needs of our customers. I want to understand how work in Purchasing to keep a good credit rating and avoid spending too much or buying the wrong things contributes to meeting these important considerations.

You tell me that all three are essential if we're to stay in business—that without good credit, smart purchasing, and getting the most for the least we're not going to remain profitable; that our customers rely on us to make things on schedule; and that nothing is worse than a bad credit rating to scare away a potential new customer. All this makes sense, and I write down your responses carefully before asking if there are any specific company goals that might sum all this up and tie these risks and concerns to one or more of the company's major objectives. Your response is to simply say, "Customer satisfaction is our primary objective."

That phrase is on every wall of the plant, appears on colorful banners in each of the employee lounges, and is the first item discussed every month at the managers' business status meeting. It's now clear that the work of the Purchasing department is designed to take care of several things: a primary company objective, customer concerns, and defined risks. What better foundation could there be to examine the purchasing plan to see how these important concerns are managed?

But before taking that step I'd like to know a few more things, such as who the primary players are within the department, and to whom they report. It's going to be important to know these things as I work within your department, so now's the time to lay the groundwork and try to understand the players' names and positions. (All along the way, I'll be collecting names and positions for another reason, but we'll learn why soon enough.)

Okay, with the players, risks, and customer connection understood, I now ask if you'd talk me through a general description of how the purchasing process works. It needn't be all that complicated. For now, I just want to have a general sense of how things are done in your department. As you describe the flow of events, paperwork, locations, and concerns, I try my best to write a brief summary in order to repeat it back to you, much as I would if I'd asked you for directions to a downtown hotel. This is the basic plan; we'll get more specific as the audit progresses.

Of course, much of what you just told me is also what is done in the department, so we naturally are drawn to those activities. I'll be looking for where your department gets its orders to proceed and what is done once those orders arrive. As a PDCA auditor, I understand those orders as input to the purchasing process, and I'm very interested in whether that input is well received or if there are any nagging problems. If the work is never held up or complicated by a lack of specifics; if the machinery, computers, tools, and other equipment you use is never a problem; or if you or a purchasing agent later tells me that customers are calling every day thanking the department for the wonderful work it does—I'll be happy to conclude that PDCA is working well and recommend special accommodation in my audit report. But if I hear differently, I want to be sure to make note of the issue and investigate how or why the problems came about in the first place.

Now on to the checking functions within your department. How do you know that the risks you mentioned at the beginning of the audit are actually being managed? What checks are normally taken to ensure that all is working according to plan? How often do you perform these checks, and how many people, including top management, get to see the results of those checks? In managing the stated risks, it's important to learn whether these checks are true indicators of success versus needed improvement. For example, if you told me that every week you check the amount of money that cycled through your department, and that you get a sales report every 2 weeks, I'd then ask you exactly how those reports provide measurement details about the three risks you mentioned earlier: spending too much for the things the company buys, ordering the wrong things and thereby slowing or stopping production, and keeping the company's credit rating intact.

The check function of PDCA is not about someone else's work. It's about regularly determining whether a specific plan is working and utilizing a true measurement of success toward a goal or set of goals. If your checks aren't appropriate for determining your product's quality or your ability to manage known risks, the odds are that your department is unaware of its true performance and therefore is less able to improve.

I'm really looking for *objective evidence* during the checking phase of a PDCA audit. Checks often come in the form of records. Your Purchasing department probably has incoming inspection records and all sorts of paperwork that has to be approved from time to time. Each is as much a check as would be a monthly report to management in which your three risks were defined and measurements based on performance to a goal were described. I want to find these records to discover performance issues you think are worth checking in your department and to take me to the last phase of my audit.

What are you doing about it? Let's say that costs are going through the roof and each month you are reporting this fact to top management. Obviously the plan to control your number one risk—spending too much for the things the company buys—is in trouble. You identified the risk and put a process in place to manage it, but now that you've checked, it's clearly not working as you expected. Again, what are you doing about it? What action will you take to resolve this problem, to revise the original plan, or perhaps to start over with an entirely new plan to better control the cost of the things you buy? I'm searching for a happy ending to this journey by finding a complete PDCA cycle within the purchasing operation that's understood by as many as possible within the department and elsewhere.

Along the way, I'll talk to people who use some of the products that are purchased by your department. I'll ask them if they are satisfied with the quality of these things and if they are satisfied with the company's overall purchasing system. And, yes, I'll also take down their names and job titles. I might ask to see something recently processed through Purchasing to work my way back through the paperwork and thereby trace the process you described to me. I could do this several times from different places within the company, to determine if everyone was following the same process plan and getting much the same level of responsiveness. I'd be collecting good evidence to relate to you and your staff at the closing meeting about how well the overall process appeared to be working. (A closing meeting is traditionally held at the end of an audit with all interested parties in attendance.)

But why collect names and titles? Because before that closing meeting I'd take a side trip to the Human Resources department and ask about each of those people. I'd want to know if they had the proper authority and were assigned responsibility for the areas in which they were working when I spoke with them. If I could learn even more about them without violating privacy laws, all the better to allow me to say positive things about them at the closing meeting. I want to be sure I was talking to people who were truly competent to discuss these issues with me during the audit. That's why I wrote down names and made sure to check their credentials before I made my final report.

The closing meeting would be a summary of what I found and little else. Was there evidence of PDCA and improvement? Were the risks and objectives well managed using PDCA? Did I find any lingering problems that were discovered during a previous audit or a nonconformance that's still not resolved? Are inputs, transformations of those inputs into outputs, and checks for effectiveness well defined and telling the company what it needs to improve? Were there any clear weaknesses as well as any exceptionally fine work noted during the audit?

This would be the end of our Purchasing audit, one in which I would have learned a great deal about your department and how it impacts areas within the company and, hopefully, our customers. But take a minute and think about the process I used to conduct this PDCA audit. It was completely generic! Each question I raised could've been asked of anyone in any department. Each question was appropriate to any subject, any area, or any individual. In the end, our imaginary Purchasing audit makes clear that PDCA is universal in its application and represents the perfect arrangement of steps in an auditor's journey, regardless of the destination. The questions asked of you as a purchasing manager would've been just as effective if they'd been asked of a line worker, a maintenance mechanic, or the president of your company. Let's list them in a general manner to get the idea:

1. What are the risks of not doing your work effectively—or put another way, what risks are avoided through the work you normally do?

2. Of what importance are these risks to the company and to our customers?

3. Is there a company objective or objectives that relate directly to your work?

4. Who is in charge, and who reports to whom?

5. What is it that you actually do?

6. Where do you get the information, input, or message to actually start doing what you do?

7. Is everything going well, or are there problems that just don't seem to go away?

8. Are the tools you're using working as well as expected?

9. Where does your work go when you're through, what is it used for, and who gets it to do their work?

10. What sort of measurements are you using to check whether you're doing a good job of managing those risks?

11. What are those measurements telling you and what are you doing about it?

Finally, I'll go to the places that had sent their output to the department I was auditing as well as to the place that received the audited department's work. I'll also ask them some of the same questions, especially whether they have any problems with the output of the audited department and if the tools they use are working well. Then it's off to the HR department to look over job descriptions and to make sure certifications and whatever minimal stated experience and skills are confirmed for each person I've talked to during the audit.

The audit is generic, but very much process driven. After all, we've learned the following:

- Why the work is important

- Where the workers get their input

- What they do to transform that input into output

- What they do to check whether the work is acceptable

- Whether those checks indicate if things are improving

- Where their work goes

- Whether it is acceptable as input to the next process in the chain

- Whether throughout the process resources are performing as expected

- Whether the people doing the work are competent

ISO 9001:2000 is filled with excellent business practices that range from documentation controls to preventive action, most of which are generic elements. Continuous improvement, for example, is expected throughout the organization, not just in one or two departments. Within PDCA, continuous improvement is an act function, something that is the output of analyzing what's been checked. ISO 9001:2000 also requires that processes be measured for effectiveness, but certainly no one would expect this requirement to apply only to a few processes within your organization. In the PDCA cycle, measuring is a check.

All those generic elements, as each is a part of every process, must therefore also represent a plan, do, check, or act function.

Imagine if those generic elements were classified according to their PDCA functions and then arranged so as to lead an auditor through a series of ISO 9001:2000 PDCA questions. The result would be a generic ISO 9001:2000 audit. Our Purchasing audit would ask essentially the same questions, but now they would be drawn from, or linked to, the standard itself. Described in the next chapter, that's exactly what the PDCA Audit Master was designed to accomplish. This tool is used in every PDCA audit and takes its questions from all the generic elements of the standard that relate to planning, doing, checking, and acting. It is simultaneously global and local in its approach without complicating the audit process, due to the manner in which the questions are arranged and structured. Finally, it is the auditor's new frame of reference that accompanies him on all subsequent audits to ensure that his work addresses P, D, C, and A wherever the auditor's journey may lead.

8

The PDCA Audit Master: The Generic ISO 9001:2000 PDCA Audit Tool

The complete PDCA Audit Master is contained in Appendix A. We'll go through it here, one segment at a time, so be prepared to flip between sections of the book as you follow along. We'll start with the opening statement on the front cover, page 1 of the Audit Master. Read it now and come back when you're finished.

PAGE 1

The day may come when your third-party auditor will question your approach. Although ISO 9001:2000 carries the expectation of process auditing, it is still early in the evolution and universal understanding of the technique. These few paragraphs go a long way in describing the PDCA approach to process auditing and may come in handy as a guide to explain this system to others. You also may have noticed that the Audit Master is built primarily on sections 4.1 and 7.1, sections we described previously as addressing the global and local concerns of any process within a system. In the pages that follow, as you learn about using the Audit Master's four parts and their subsections, take note of just how important these two ISO 9001:2000 elements are to a successful audit.

Their significance comes from their ability to apply PDCA to both the overall system and the individual processes that make up that system. For the most part, your audits will normally be focused on examination of one or more processes, but the Audit Master will help you incorporate the larger picture and thereby identify where the individual process helps or hinders the overall system. An internal audit program that accomplishes this objective on a regular basis is adding real value to the organization because correcting problems locally has a positive effect globally. Over time, those improvements add up to real gains that are noticed throughout the organization, its customers and suppliers.

PART I: PLAN

Part I has four sections because if a plan is to be effective and lead to improvement, it must consider all four of the PDCA functions prior to implementation. Section 1 is concerned with why the plan was developed in the first place. It sets the tone of the audit by asking the person being audited about his or her work in an interesting manner, one that will also define the course of the audit in the process.

Section 1: Motivation and Risk

As you examine the questions in section 1, remember the generic Purchasing audit in the previous chapter. You can readily see how these questions mirror the questions from that audit—but now they are drawn from specific ISO 9001:2000 elements. Notice the elements are listed by ISO section number just to the right of the heading. These five questions in section 1 and all the others in Part I address elements 4.1(a)–4.1(e), 5.1(c), 5.2, 5.4.2(a), 6.2.2(d), 7.1(a)–7.1(d), 8.1, and 8.2.3 of the standard. As with all audit questions, the skilled auditor will try not to parrot the standard, but rather will try to connect with the person being audited using his or her own words. In fact, the PDCA Audit Master is not to be considered as a written representation of the one and only way to address each question. If that were true, the audit process would soon become just another "checklist" audit, something you want to avoid if the audit function in your organization is to grow and provide greater depth and value. The best audit is one that flows from one question to the next in the auditor's own words to make the experience as natural as possible. If you feel awkward asking any question in the Audit Master, especially when prior questions have already covered the same ground, it's important to maintain the flow of conversation by rephrasing or simply moving on to the next question.

Section 2: Process Plan

Section 2 of Part I consists of a brief series of questions designed to put the audit subject at ease, to begin the process of understanding what takes place within the area you're auditing. We'll explain what is meant by the directive to "Plug in PDCA Plan questions here" in the next chapter. For now, read through the questions and imagine that you're simply having a conversation with someone and that you're truly interested in how she plans for the work that comes to her on any given day. As she tells her story, you are writing down the chain of events she describes in broad terms and occasionally asking if you've got everything right by repeating what you've written. This is especially important when the level of detail is high and it's coming at you rapidly. Take the time to digest what you've heard and do your best to paraphrase the important points clearly when you're ready.

Section 3: Key Players

Section 3 is the "Who's Who" of a PDCA audit. Getting the names and position descriptions of the key people you meet along the way expands every audit to examine compliance with section 6.2.2 ("Employee Competence") of the ISO 9001:2000 Standard. Look carefully at the last sentence in italics: *"Note any big differences as Observations or Findings if there are no records of competence such as evaluations, certificates, training records, etc."* We'll explain the mechanics of findings and observations in the next chapter; however, it's easy to understand that the organization is at risk if the people who manage or produce the products and services that directly impact the customer's perception of quality are lacking the necessary skills, training, education, and experience to meet those expectations. Auditing the human as well as the tangible resources of your company or organization strikes a logical balance in the pursuit of overall excellence. A large part of the plan to meet customer expectations is the development of the people within the organization. As an internal PDCA auditor, you are not only in search of the plan to define and develop human assets, but also to seek the measurement and improvement of both as the system matures by acting on what it learns about its performance over time. (PDCA!)

Section 4: Evaluation Method

Section 4 is the first series of questions designed to probe how the audited process is routinely checked to determine if it is meeting the needs and managing the risks previously discussed. But notice that after each question is another directive in italics: *"Get records!"* It's time to start collecting hard evidence. Many of the typical checks of process effectiveness are contained in test reports, inspection records, satisfaction surveys, management reports, statistical analysis, cost of (poor) quality reports, efficiency numbers, charts, and other data. Ask for copies whenever possible. They will ultimately be attached to the audit report to help others understand and/or serve as evidence of how you arrived at your conclusions. They are also important as you attempt to truly understand their process and concerns. Having the audited individual explain these reports and measures is most often a mutual learning experience, especially in context of the Audit Master's approach to these measurements in the first place.

As you review these four questions, imagine how prior responses to questions in sections 1, 2, and 3 now require an element of action and follow-through, coupled with a request for evidence. The audit is no longer theoretical or intangible. Your investigation of the overall plan is clearly at the stage where you would expect something to surface that indicates either success or needed improvement. Find whatever it is and, whenever possible, save it as a record. This last section of Part I serves as a foundation for the rest of the audit. Combined, each section in Part I has prepared you for what's to come by defining what's important, what's being done to protect against risk, who is responsible, and what sort of tools are used to monitor progress.

The Big Picture

The remaining Audit Master sections, Do, Check, and Act, also contain generic ISO 9001:2000 elements. It would be helpful at this point to list all these generic or universal PDCA ISO 9001:2000 elements to demonstrate how PDCA auditing automatically draws the auditor into an examination of multiple elements within the standard:

Plan: 4.1a–e, 5.1c, 5.2, 5.4.2a, 6.2.2d, 7.1a–d, 8.1, 8.2.3

Do: 4.1b, 4.1d, 7.1b, 7.5.1a–f, 7.5.2, 8.5.1

Check: 4.1e, 8.4, 8.2.1

Act: 4.1f, 5.4.2b, 5.6, 7.1d, 7.2.3, 8.2.2, 8.5.1–3

These ISO 9001:2000 elements are secondary to the PDCA auditing process. We're no longer auditing to determine compliance to the standard. Instead we're auditing a department of function in the organization and taking the standard along as we ask about the PDCA components within that area.

The standard is going along for the ride, not telling us where to go!

PART II: DO

Part II usually requires a bit of travel and discovery. We already know what actually gets done from several of the questions in Part I. Now, we want to witness what was described to us. Part II is divided into three sections: Process Inputs, Work Plan, and Process Outputs.

Section 1: Process Inputs

Section 1 is looking for evidence of clear and understandable process inputs. We want to collect evidence wherever possible because we're also hoping to go to the place where that evidence was originally created. Let's use the Purchasing audit once again as an example to illustrate this point.

The first question in section 1 of Part II asks for output from a previous function or department that serves as an input to the Purchasing department. Imagine that you're shown a copy of a purchase requisition and perhaps a recent printout of a software program that automatically sends requests for materials to vendors once the order is placed by Customer Service. You've now got the evidence you need to backtrack the process, or "swim upstream," to investigate the input source.

Notice that the Audit Master once again indents and underlines suggested instructions for later activities. In this case, and as a final activity at the end of Part II, those questions simply inquire about how work is received and if there's anything that might be improved in the handoff between departments. This is a great opportunity to examine the quality of the work that serves as input to the department you're auditing. The same thing takes place at the end of Part II when you're asked to visit the output, if possible, of the function or department you're auditing.

When a PDCA auditor visits the input and output points of a process, it's not at all uncommon to walk into a whole new set of issues in need of improvement. Systemic weaknesses can be expected. For example, imagine a relay race. At the start, the runners are out of the blocks, each sprinting ahead to position themselves as the front-runner when the baton pass is made to their next team member. In relay racing that's everyone's process or objective: to start fast, stay fast, and be in front at the baton exchange. However, between each runner is another process that's shared: the baton exchange itself. A lot of practice is typically applied to make the exchange process work well, especially to eliminate dropping the baton or slowing the pace of the runners in any manner. The baton represents the output of the first runner and the input to the next. Did it arrive in time? Were there any problems in delivering the baton to the next runner? Was the baton handed off as practiced, or were there unexpected issues that made the exchange more difficult?

Just as the Purchasing department passes purchased materials to the intended recipient, so too do the Scheduling and Sales departments pass their information along to the Purchasing people. The evidence or paperwork you collect is the same as the baton—it represents the input and/or output of the departments within the system you're auditing. Investigating the handoffs, where one process provides input to the next process in the system, is a primary strength of a PDCA audit.

Section 2: Work Plan

As you read through the questions in section 2, remember that your intent as the PDCA auditor is to encourage the interviewee to explain the value and/or difficulties encountered with the tools she uses and how they are performing. In an office setting, this might include computers and copy machines, while on the plant floor there are all manner of machines and devices that come into play during an average day's work.

Section 3: Process Outputs

Section 3 is all about output and whether what is sent to the next process is checked sufficiently before it is passed to the next in line. Once again, there's another underlined and indented section that's designed to test the perception of quality by the department that receives the work you're auditing. In section 1 ("Process Inputs"), I said that this is a great opportunity to examine the quality of the work that serves as input to the department you're auditing. Now, the same is true of the opportunity you're given to examine the quality of the processes output.

PART III: CHECK

There's only one section to Part III, and it's all about performance and measurement. Notice that there are several questions about what happens with the information after something is checked. Is this information shared with top management in a timely manner? Do others within the organization have an opportunity to also learn, perhaps to improve, from what's been discovered? The ISO 9001:2000 Standard is all about improvement and communication, so it stands to reason that information based on fact would be encouraged as much as the subsequent advantages of trying to apply solid information in as many levels as possible within the company.

The fourth (and toughest) question in this section is about performance criteria and whether the parameters for measurement were altered from the original plan. Too often, the rules change after the agreement to proceed has been decided. Top management allocated resources based on the original criteria, however, and to alter the type, frequency, scope, or metrics at some point afterward is not in keeping with that original agreement.

When you approach this question, think about what you were told in Part I, section 4 ("Evaluation Method"). The evidence you collected there is a good starting place at this stage of the audit to review in greater detail. Are the data and the information that those data created the same as originally conceived, or has suboptimal performance or some unexpected glitch caused the numbers to be collected less frequently than originally planned? Has the success of the program been so overwhelming that the department no longer bothers to check on its performance as originally agreed? In time, each of these lapses in checking will present barriers to continuous improvement—even in a success situation that in time might fail to notice slipping sales or customer discontent as the product and its market mature. Take time to learn whether the criteria have changed. The most significant discovery of the audit might be that the agreed-upon checks were downplayed or discontinued.

PART IV: ACT

The end of the PDCA loop is also the end of the audit. Here is where the value should be found, the logical improvements that ought to have arisen as a result of checking on how well the plan was able to meet its expectations. Of course, the Audit Master's questions reflect the general things that one would hope to find:

What evidence is available of action(s) for improvement or revision of the original plan?

There must be something to show for all the work that's been done. The checks, reports, and analysis (hopefully shared with members of the department and top management) clarified something that, in turn, was acted upon. What was it, and where is the evidence of its having taken place? Was the plan modified? Was the outcome so good that the improvement was shared with others so that they might also improve their operations? Let's see it! Where is it and how is it going?

Based on performance analysis, what resources were redistributed to better manage risk or to achieve the desired outcome?

Acting on the information provided by checking changed things one way or another. The most obvious change is to the type and amount of additional resources available or needed after the plan has had its chance to work. If all went really well, perhaps the people in that department can now concentrate on new levels of quality. They are now able to do more with less and their output continues to increase. Their resource demands are less and their productivity has improved. The evidence will be there in some format, perhaps the "before and after" efficiency numbers placed side by side with the overtime records for the same period. A search for the answer to this question will be of great interest to top management.

They are ultimately responsible for the company's resources, and audit reports that share resource information help them to better comprehend the result of their decisions.

What has been the customer's reaction to these revisions?

The true test of any process improvement is in the customer's awareness and support of the change. Amazingly simple, but far too often taken for granted, is the question that has the greatest overall impact on the organization: Does the customer care? If not, all the PDCA in the world cannot create exclusively internal improvement nor avoid ultimately being brought down by customers who never cared or wanted the change in the first place. The customer is the last word—not the ledger sheet, not the glowing internal review, and not the improved efficiency reports. Whether it's a survey, testimonials, a focus group, or a carefully planned series of customer tests and evaluations, the word on the street should match all the congratulations in the shop for a job well done.

It was once said of a very famous designer that his creations were the result of watching the expressions of those who attended his competitors' fashion shows. If certain styles brought a frown, he steered away from that design. The result of his "research" would be brought out later at his show, where he performed the very same exercise with his own fashions. If he saw fewer frowns and more smiles, he knew that he'd read his customers correctly, and record sales soon followed. In his own way, the designer followed pure PDCA in carrying out his plan. But instead of just doing the research and building the wardrobe collection, he then followed it through to the point where he could see it working on his customers' faces. A good auditor will want to know not only that the plan worked, but also whether the customer is smiling.

Did top management review any of these revisions before they were implemented? Did they consider (discuss or ask about) operational issues in relation to other processes in the system? Are there records of the decision to revise the process?

The question may be a mouthful, but the point is relatively simple. Does top management know what's going on? Did they review what the improvement plan involved by examining performance data or other facts before any action was taken? If they did, get a record of the review as objective evidence that it took place. They need to know what's involved because an action in one place can, and often does, have an effect on another. Top managers are in the best position to see the big picture, so it's their responsibility to look at the entire operation before approving change in any one area. If too many changes are allowed to act on any system without sufficient oversight and planned integration, the result is chaos and its attendant loss of output, responsiveness, and growth. The evidence may be in quality council or management review minutes, special announcements and letters, or even in the approvals necessary for purchases to implement a proposed change.

PART V: SUPPORTING AUDIT PROCESSES

Part V is concerned with audits, corrective action, and documentation. If there was a previous audit, it stands to reason that the issues raised during that experience are worth reinvestigating. Previous audits, their evidence, and the people encountered along the way are a window into the upcoming audit. Many of the places and characters will repeat themselves this time around, but hopefully with greater levels of success and confidence in their process.

Nonconformances and corrective actions that arose from them are also worthy of a second look to see if everything turned out as planned. In fact, including any corrective actions in an audit is a *verification* step: something that's vital to ensuring that the root cause was truly addressed and controlled. Auditors add prior audit findings as well as corrective and preventive actions to the list of questions and issues they will investigate, to report back whether they were worth the paper they were printed on. The best of intentions and training are too often the universal answers to things that go wrong in organizations. Unfortunately, once they have been exhausted, the willingness to believe they've worked takes over. The auditor is looking for evidence, not hope, that the nonconformance cannot occur again following an effort to correct it.

Documentation is a subject in and of itself—but for the purpose of a PDCA audit, we want to first look through the company's ISO 9001:2000 documentation to determine what's relevant to the upcoming audit and study it closely. If we were to audit Purchasing, we might find a purchasing process or certainly mention of the purchasing procedure in the Quality Manual. Each piece of available information makes the auditor that much more capable of asking intelligent questions. Documentation is a window to the world the auditor is about to enter, so better to look through it and be prepared. Learning about a department's processes is surprisingly easy in most operations. What they do, whether they require any certifications or special licenses, how they check things, and what reports they use are typically to be found in job descriptions, if not directly in the department's own work instructions and training materials. The point is that not everything is handily available in controlled ISO process documentation. Often, the auditor's journey must explore any number of outlets for written descriptions of what he or she will encounter along the way.

PART VI: AUDIT SUMMARY

The Audit Master is really separated into two major functions: the audit questions and evidence collected along the way, and the Audit Summary, a single-page description of the audit for top management. Top management reviews and uses data as their raw material. It is the fuel that drives their decisions. They are expected to use their intelligence, experience, and training to make a proper decision in much the same manner as a line worker is expected to produce a part from steel, heat, and pressure. Both workers and top management need only enough raw materials to do exactly what is required in the most efficient manner. If there's an unnecessarily large amount of material, time is wasted in managing it instead of managing the work of converting it into a finished product. Workers moving steel or trying to find places to work between stacks of metal aren't making parts. And top managers reading unnecessarily long reports are not making decisions efficiently either.

The Audit Summary is not an outlet for creative writing, and certainly not a place for oratory and opinion. The auditor is grounded by the ISO 9001:2000 Standard. Every statement, especially those involving a negative situation, must be referenced to the numbered element of the standard and/or the internal document it refers to. If the Purchasing department has no program to monitor supplier performance, it's a violation of section 7.4.1 and should be stated as such in the report. But, on the other hand, if the temperament of the purchasing manager was less than warm and friendly when the matter was brought to her attention, the matter will remain outside the Audit Summary.

Be specific and stick to the big issues. While it may be true that during the audit there were seven instances of minor importance, those three major process violations are far more important to controlling the real risks to the organization and must be the focal point of the report. Be blunt, be brief, and be accurate.

A good report will begin with an overview of the general state of affairs. Most of the time, this is the place to say something positive about the audited department and its staff. No matter what was discovered in the audit, it's always possible to lead with a good word or two about something the auditor encountered during the journey. When discussing findings and observations, always identify the ISO element that applies to the issue or situation. For example, if the company has not identified the key processes within its operating system, the internal auditor's finding would best read as follows:

4.1(a) – There was no available evidence that the organization has defined the processes that make up the Ajax Services operating system.

The ISO 9001:2000 element is clearly indicated at the beginning of the sentence. Top management will therefore be addressing the need to comply with the element, not the auditor's opinion. It's an important distinction because the auditor is not to have an opinion in these matters. The strength of ISO 9001:2000 audits is their connection to the standard, not the varying opinions of individuals. The Audit Summary is a business document, an impartial and factual account of the auditor's journey. As such, the ABCs of writing the Audit Summary are:

- Accuracy

- Brevity

- Clarity

When accuracy counts most is when a finding or observation contains factual data and information that can be used later on in developing corrective action. Brevity is the outcome of attending to the most important things and the discipline to work under the motto "Less is more." Clarity is also a discipline, one that may require several rewrites to achieve, but worth every minute of the auditor's time. Try to use the ABCs to summarize the audit in just one page. This single page should have all the information top management needs to decide what further actions might be necessary. When an Audit Summary is truly effective, it gets right to the point and provides just enough data and evidence for background and follow-up.

The finished audit, the Audit Master's series of questions and answers, the Audit Summary, and copies of collected evidence will all remain in the file for later use. We've already discussed the use of prior audits to verify corrective action arising from an earlier audit finding. And, of course, the file may also be used for background in developing the initial corrective action. Because information in the audit may be used by others at any time, neatness and legibility are important. Typing the audit is a great help toward achieving the level of professionalism that it deserves. After all the time spent developing the proper series of questions, reviewing documentation, noting corrective action, examining prior audits, and finally conducting the audit itself and developing the Audit Summary—it only makes sense to complete the work in a manner that reflects the degree of effort it required.

That effort requires one final step before the journey can begin. The Audit Master has provided a generic PDCA approach grounded in several ISO 9001:2000 elements. It's possible to use the Audit Master in any setting and arrive at a generally valid assessment of PDCA within that area. In turn, several strengths and weaknesses may become evident to the degree that the auditor can determine if one or more issues merit inclusion in the Audit Summary. But what insurance does the auditor have that he or she will be certain to ask other, more specific ISO 9001:2000–related questions?

The statement "You don't know what you don't know" contains a great deal of truth. Auditors who venture into areas of an organization that work with highly detailed processes, tools, required certifications, and other exacting issues risk failing to notice a great deal of what's specific to that area if they are prepared only with a generic series of questions. The auditor's insurance policy for completeness requires that one last step be taken before the actual journey can begin. The final chapter is also the final phase of the audit plan, where generic and specific ISO 9001:2000 requirements combine to create a truly comprehensive audit approach.

9

Integrating ISO Specifics into the Audit

The Audit Master's primary strength is also its greatest weakness. Its generic approach makes it possible to include ISO 9001:2000 PDCA elements in every audit. Especially in those places where traditional audits typically examine only what is done in a given process, the Audit Master's comprehensive PDCA approach extends the scope to include planning, measurement, and improvement. Unfortunately, the world is not generic, and neither are all the elements within the standard. Therefore, by itself, the Audit Master is much too broad for a truly comprehensive audit and needs to be expanded to include specific elements when the auditor's journey extends into those special places.

What places? A partial list would include Design, Calibration, Corrective Action, Document Control, and Management Review. And there are more. The point is that most audits are about a specific function, topic, department, or process, and in all probability each is addressed directly in the standard. We've been using Purchasing as an example, and it is also one of those special places where the standard requires the auditor to explore particular issues such as supplier selection criteria and performance feedback. The generic Audit Master does not address these important specifics, and for an audit of Purchasing to be fully comprehensive, this and other Purchasing elements must therefore be added. The same is true in all the other places where ISO 9001:2000 gets specific.

But how can the generic Audit Master retain its PDCA flow and direction when confronted by the need to include additional specific planning, doing, checking, and acting functions? Exactly where in the PDCA audit does the auditor plug in these separate and often very detailed specifics? How will an auditor quickly determine, for example, whether the subject of supplier selection criteria is a P, D, C, or A activity and structure the audit to make this inquiry at the proper time?

THE ISO 9001:2000 PDCA GUIDE

Another tool is clearly required to help make these decisions, and the ISO 9001:2000 PDCA Guide was designed exclusively to accomplish this important work. In a nutshell, the PDCA Guide identifies each ISO 9001:2000 element as a Plan, Do, Check, or Act activity. We've already discussed all the generic PDCA elements in our examination of the Audit Master. The PDCA Guide picks up where the Audit Master left off and provides the auditor with an easy reference for placement of additional specific questions within the appropriate Plan, Do, Check, or Act sections of the Audit Master.

Not only does the PDCA Guide provide coded references to all elements of the standard, but it also offers several other auditor-friendly features to develop a comprehensive internal audit. Refer to Appendix B as you read through the following feature descriptions of the PDCA Guide.

PDCA

Each element is coded as a Plan, Do, Check, or Act activity or function. These are to be found in the far left-hand column on each page of the guide. Planning elements are to be added to section 2 of Part I in the Audit Master. You may remember the phrase "Plug in PDCA Plan questions here" from Chapter 8's description of this section—and we stated that we would follow up at a later time. Now is that time. The purpose of inserting new specific planning elements in this section of the Audit Master is to maintain the PDCA flow within the audit. Planning questions from the PDCA Guide inserted in section 2 work alongside the generic planning questions already in place in the Audit Master. The remaining parts of the Audit Master are free to accept additional questions anywhere within their respective Do, Check, or Act sections. Only section 2 (Plan) asks for additional planning specifics to be placed within it; the others are open to best placement by the auditor just as long as they harmonize with their generic Do, Check, or Act questions already contained within the Audit Master.

Bottom-of-Page Legend

The legend at the bottom of each page identifies three additional features designed to help the auditor recognize important interconnections and requirements:

✎   *Documented Procedures:* The ISO 9001:2000 Standard requires documented procedures for six elements: Documentation, Records, Auditing, Nonconformance, Corrective Action, and Preventive Action. The PDCA Guide makes note of these critical areas to alert the auditor to examine any that might apply to an upcoming audit. In truth, each is usually relevant in every audit. Each department has documentation and records of some variety. It is important to examine those that are revision controlled, to determine if the process they utilize is as described in the written documentation procedure. Similarly, any records that the department keeps should be managed and stored in the manner described in the written procedure for records. Of course, the documented internal audit process must apply to the audit itself, so it should be reviewed periodically to be sure that the written procedure is being followed. As for the remaining three required written processes, the previous chapter made clear that any prior nonconformance, corrective, or preventive action should be investigated during the audit—but now the auditor can also check to see if these records indicate adherence to their documented procedures as well. Were they processed as documented? Were there any lapses in thoroughness or required communications? The opportunity to review each documented procedure could be thought of as "an audit within an audit." Should review of these six documented processes take place prior to every audit? Not necessarily. In time, the nonconformance procedure will become well known by the auditing staff and they'll recognize any omissions or deviations from existing documentation. The same is true of all the other procedures for which documentation is required. Review of previous audits and nonconformances will always be an element of every audit, however. Verification of effectiveness is an important value-added component of internal auditing.

Required Process: The auditor's journey is much like any vacation in one critical area. When people return from vacations they are usually eager to share pictures and other evidence of their trip. Records are evidence of adherence to process and performance, just as snapshots are evidence of particularly interesting places and things. Collecting copies of records, however, carries deeper requirements than are already suggested in the Audit Master. ISO 9001:2000 requires specific records to be in place in every organization, and the PDCA Guide highlights each of these by drawing a rectangle around them. When auditors find themselves visiting these areas, they should ask to see these records and should make copies whenever possible for inclusion in the audit report. If copies are not permitted, auditors should summarize the content briefly by writing down the form number, who or what is the subject, the date, and any other particulars that would make possible a comprehensive subsequent reinvestigation.

In PDCA Audit Master: The Audit Master includes many elements of the standard, and without a guide it would be difficult to quickly determine whether a particular element is already included. Each of the already included elements in the Audit Master are therefore circled in the PDCA Guide to help the auditor prepare for an upcoming audit by having only to concentrate on elements specific to that audit.

The Plan of the PDCA Guide

The PDCA Guide is a reference document. Its value is as a planning tool in the development of the audit. As you review its content, be aware that the Plan, Do, Check, and Act functions listed in the far-left column are guidelines, not requirements. There are times when the setting dictates function, such as a situation where planning is actually an activity in and of itself. It's not uncommon to come across a process where the plan involves the requirement to set aside specific times and locations to conduct planning. In that setting, regular planning is actually a Do function. But don't be overly concerned. The value of the PDCA approach is in the flow of questions from one general area to the next. In that sense, any misclassification of a P, D, C, or A function has never been found to overly disrupt the audit. Instead, most confusion occurs between neighboring P, D, C, or A functions, just as in the previous example where planning was actually found to be a Do function. In these situations, the closeness of functions in the PDCA cycle serves to naturally move the audit forward. The PDCA Guide is as reliable as dependence on common sense and experience to guide you through unexplored territory. From time to time, neither is 100 percent appropriate to the situation. However, as a tool to help auditors classify elements according to their PDCA function, the PDCA Guide brings both common sense and experience to the process.

BUT THEY'RE NOT QUESTIONS!

Of all the difficult issues that beginning ISO 9001:2000 auditors confront, few are as universal as how to convert an ISO element into a good audit question.

Elements are written as statements, not questions, and for many auditors it's difficult to translate one into the other. Consider ISO 9001:2000 elements 7.5.1(a)–7.5.1(f), with all those specific requirements about work instructions and equipment. An auditor could simply run down each requirement by asking, "Do you use work instructions?" or "Do you use monitoring or measuring devices?" or "Are they available?" It's almost guaranteed that every reply will be either yes or no, isn't it? That's compliance auditing once again, and it rarely gets into the heart of the process as the audit skips from one simple answer to the next.

But how can a list of requirements as specific as those in 7.5.1 be handled in a better way? By asking a very open-ended question designed to lead the audit subject into a general discussion of her work. After all, an open-ended question is one that has no wrong answer and allows for a story to unfold—and in the process a deeper understanding is developed. A question as simple and unthreatening as "Could you tell me about the everyday work you do and the things you rely on to be sure that it's done properly?" gives the audit subject plenty of room to describe any number of things that will most likely be found as requirements in ISO 9001:2000 section 7.5. During the conversation the interviewee may show you various tools, work instructions, special fixtures, prints, computer records, and even protective clothing. In fact, the list of things you'll discover will probably be much longer than if you had asked a series of specific and directed questions.

The best audit question isn't really about ISO. It's about what's going on around you as the audit develops. The PDCA cycle is a story that should have just one ending: Either the plan worked and things improved, or it didn't work and an improved plan is in place or will soon be implemented. Find that story. Ask questions that come from what you see and hear as the audit progresses through the Plan, Do, Check, and Act phases. Learn about the place you're visiting in real time. As an auditor you have already prepared, studied, and read quite a lot about the process under investigation. This preparation should result in a unique understanding of the requirements, problems, past failures, successes, records, and documentation that should be in evidence during the audit. Why not discover these things and many others by asking questions that express interest in the process rather than compliance to the standard? Auditors who are well prepared already know the details. As much as possible, let those who are being audited supply them through their answers instead of asking about them directly.

Of all the auditor's skills that routinely appear in books and articles, patience and the ability to listen are usually somewhere near the top of the list. But patience and good listening skills are meaningless if the auditor is uninterested or not fully prepared. Preparation is a planning activity, and without disciplined preparation most audits turn out to be either superficial and of little value or laborious and time-consuming. No wonder, in that we've already learned the same is true for all poorly planned processes. To learn how to convert a statement into a question, learn all that you can during the planning stage of the audit itself. The more you know about the details you're hoping to uncover, the more your listening skills and patience will pay off.

THE PDCA GUIDE PLUG-IN PROCESS

During your audit preparation, you should have the Audit Master on one side of your desktop and the PDCA Guide and a copy of the ISO 9001:2000 Standard on the other. First, look through the ISO 9001:2000 Standard and make note of all the elements that relate directly to the operation, process, function, or department that you will be auditing. For those new to the ISO 9001:2000 Standard, the table of contents is an invaluable asset in this search. Read through each selected element to be sure it's relevant to the upcoming audit, as several elements may overlap or appear to be appropriate but upon inspection are intended for other activities.

Once the relevant sections are determined, open the PDCA Audit Guide and make note of each chosen element's PDCA function. Also, take note of any circled elements already included in the Audit Master. While these will not require any additional work because they were previously integrated, it's valuable to notice their importance in the audit. Taking the time to study each of these will also affirm your increasing ability to see the big picture. Because the Audit Master is composed of generic PDCA elements, the more of these an auditor identifies indicates a growing awareness of collective application and comprehensiveness regardless of the audit subject.

With the Audit Master now ready for addition of specific ISO 9001:2000 elements for the upcoming audit, it's time to insert these into their proper P, D, C, or A sections. Planning questions are added to Part I, section 2. If we were auditing Purchasing, for instance, the PDCA Guide includes several planning elements, most in section 7.4.2 ("Purchasing Information").

Section 7.4.2(a) wants to know if information is available for requirements of approval of products, procedures, processes, and equipment. It takes planning to generate this information, and it may be housed in several places, each of which was carefully planned to allow for the information to be used easily. Section 7.4.2(b) requires planning to develop any special requirements for personnel qualifications, while 7.4.2(c) wants to see information containing the plan that explains Purchasing and its contribution to meeting requirements of the quality management system.

The auditor now translates these three elements into one or more questions within the list of questions in Part I, section 2. Use the back of the page or create a new page to allow for space to record the reply. However, these additional questions must be identified as having originated from

7.4.2(a)–7.4.2(c). Questions that are simply stated without their ISO 9001:2000 identifiers could be perceived as an auditor's personal concerns. So that there's no doubt that all audit questions are based on ISO 9001:2000, be sure to indicate the additional element's number somewhere beside the question. The example below illustrates this approach:

Section 2: Process Plan   *(Plug in PDCA Plan questions here)*
(ISO 9001:2000 Sections 4.1(a), 4.1(b), 7.1(b)–7.1(d), 6.2.2(d))

Please describe how the Purchasing process works in general terms. Are the risks you mentioned earlier managed well through what you just described to me?

What other parts of the operation benefit from the success of Purchasing?

Can you demonstrate how the Purchasing process and its performance are understood by the Purchasing staff? Is any of this recorded in verification, validation, monitoring, and inspection records?

7.4.2 – What type of information and/or information systems are utilized to clearly identify the important requirements of the products we purchase, such as:
- (a)   Requirements for approval of product, processes, and equipment?

- (b)   Requirements that certain personnel are qualified to purchase, approve, or inspect things, such as special certifications, education, or skills?

- (c)   Requirements of our quality management system?

General: Before contacting the supplier, how do we determine any specific purchase requirements?

The remaining Purchasing specifics fall into the Do, Check, and Act functions. Starting with Do, the PDCA Guide identifies the following element (7.4.1):

> The organization shall evaluate and select suppliers based on their ability to supply product in accordance with the organization's requirements. Criteria for selection, evaluation, and reevaluation shall be established.

Part II of the Audit Master carries no requirement to place this element in any particular section; however, the next-to-last question in section 1 comes close to asking about supplier selection and evaluation criteria insomuch as it's addressing controls. (When Purchasing does a good job of selecting and monitoring suppliers it's applying controls designed to reduce many of the normal supply risks of price, service, delivery, and performance quality.) So, although the element could be introduced anywhere in Part II, it's now inserted just below the next-to-last question:

Part II: Do

Section 1: Process Inputs
(ISO 9001:2000 Sections 4.1(b), 4.1(d), 7.5.1(a)–7.5.1(f))

What are the outputs of previous processes that are brought to Purchasing? *(What serves as input to start processing an order? Get evidence!)*

At a later time in the audit, go to the department(s) or function(s) whose output was input to this department as discovered above. Ask this department if what they send is well received, or is improvement/revision desired?

Is this input analyzed upon arrival to Purchasing. Are there records of this activity? *(Get copies or write down names, dates, PO #'s, etc., as objective proof.)*

What controls are applied to the Purchasing Process? *(You're looking for work instructions, prints, budgets, etc. Remember to get evidence!)*

7.4.1 – What criteria are used to select, evaluate, and reevaluate our suppliers? And how do these evaluation and selection criteria improve their ability to supply products that meet our requirements?

Are inputs received properly and well managed? *(Are there problems managing the things that you need to do your job?)*

DOUBLE DUTY ELEMENTS

The remaining PDCA functions of Check and Act specific to Purchasing are inserted in parts III and IV of the Audit Master, but this example allows us to explain another facet of PDCA and the PDCA Guide. Notice that in the PDCA Guide, section 7.4.3 ("Verification of Purchased Product") is coded as both a Check and an Act function. Here's what it says:

> The organization shall establish and implement the inspection or other activities necessary for ensuring that purchased product meets specified purchase requirements.

The subject is incoming inspection. When the purchased products arrive, the standard is pointing out that it would be a good idea to inspect the materials before accepting them into the system. We do this whenever we receive a package at home, and if there's something wrong such as damage during shipping, we may not accept it. In other words, we are checking (is everything okay?) and then acting (accept or return the package). The standard is asking for inspection or "other activities" (Check) to make sure what was bought is worth using. In practice, however, the result of that checking function is to act in one way or another. Therefore, the PDCA Guide codes this element as both a Check and/or Act PDCA function. There are others in the PDCA Guide coded as "double duty" elements and they often involve inspection requirements.

INSPECTIONS AND ACTING ON THEIR OUTPUT

Inspection is a checking function. It's also one of those quality terms that has fallen on disfavor as the price and effectiveness of traditional inspection practices are increasingly questioned. The thinking goes that the less inspection, the more time there will be to make or do things that add value and produce results. But if something must be inspected, at the very least the inspection should provide something that can be acted upon as a result. Inspected products are either shipped or not shipped based on the inspection results. Incoming products from suppliers are inspected to ensure that they meets all requirements and are either used or not used based on the inspection results. The value of required inspections, in other words, is the knowledge it provides to act on the results of those inspections. One without the other is meaningless, especially in the event that an organization spends resources on inspection and testing, but simply files the data away and never applies the results to filtering or improvement efforts.

ACT

Unfortunately, it's too often the case that inspection records are left to be little more than data. In fact, many of the checking functions within all processes are often next to ignored. This topic was discussed earlier in the book and deserves mention once again as the process of developing the complete Audit Master nears conclusion. Be prepared to dig for the answers to how the organization acted on information that arose from testing, inspection, and other checking functions. And remember to collect evidence wherever possible.

So, now that all the specific elements are added to the Audit Master, research is completed, and copies of nonconformance, prior audits, and any related corrective and preventive actions have been reviewed, the auditor is ready to alert the audit subjects and begin the audit. It will be a Process Driven Comprehensive Audit because it was carefully developed to audit all the PDCA functions, both generic and specific, that apply to the audit subject. The audit itself is a carefully planned check of the overall health of the audited department. As such, its output, the Executive Summary found on the last page of the Audit Master, is the same as any inspection record. It can be used or ignored. If it is used as the basis for action to revise the original plan, the audit was a success. If not, the audit team would be advised to do what's necessary to understand why something wasn't done in response to the information they presented to top management. Were resources unavailable? Is there another plan soon to be implemented that will correct the issues uncovered during the audit? Rather than simple indifference, there may be a very good reason why change is often slow to come in organizations.

Findings and Observations

The Audit Summary will contain information for top managers to use in making better decisions. From time to time, the auditor reports conditions that represent serious breaches of the system. It's rare, but when process controls just break down, when the written process has no relationship to observed practice and the rules were broken without concern for the consequences, the audit team must sound a clear and strong alert to call attention to the situation. These are *findings*. And although audits occasionally contain positive findings, the term is most often reserved for the big problems.

Findings are different from *observations*. Observations are of less magnitude because process controls are still in effect and/or the process is functioning as expected—there are just a few troubling omissions or an observed laxity in implementation practices. The differentiation between findings and observations, and which of these is appropriate to a given situation, is and probably will continue to be an ongoing conversation—but the following story may help to explain the difference:

It was a hot June day in 1872 as the wagon train approached the end of another day of sweat, dust, and the ever-present breakdowns of wagons and machinery. As was the custom, the wagon master sent his assistant back down the train to give instructions to the settlers for where to pull up and unload for camp that night. The process was always the same. The lead wagon began to make a slow right turn, one it made every day around this time. The cattle and other livestock were herded to the right of all the other wagons and followed along lazily, but knowingly, in anticipation of grazing and dozing as the day wound down. There would be table scraps for the dogs and treats for some of the horses, too. The circle began to take shape. Inside, the round camp area was grass covered with a small stream running through it. Prefect. Tonight would be an especially good night with hot baths, warm food, cool breezes, and a clear night sky emblazoned with stars.

Five hours of peace, good food, and company pass without incident. Everyone expresses gratitude for his or her safe westward progress thus far, and conversations turn to preparations for bed. Morning comes too quickly for a wagon train of tired settlers.

But come it does. Bright, clear, and without a single animal within the camp! They've all wandered off or were rustled away in the night. Not a one to be seen! The trail boss was first to realize the problem, quickly saddled his horse, and swore at himself as he rode off toward the other end of camp, fully expecting to find what he'd told these people over and over not to forget. The first rule of making camp is "Wagons in a Tight Circle!" and it was clear to him that somewhere, probably near or along the small stream, two of the wagons were separated far enough to allow passage for the cattle and whoever was brazen enough to sneak them through.

Sure enough, there it was. The Smithfield and the Potter wagons were at least 30 feet apart on either side of the 4-foot-wide stream. Plenty of room to quietly coax the animals through in the dead of night. Again, he swore at himself for not having his assistant check the entire camp last night. This sort of thing was always happening, and he knew it had to stop. Maybe now, with the loss of ready meat and pulling power, these settlers will finally shape up and stick to the process!

No, wait a minute—there's always room for this sort of memory lapse, especially when a camp as nice as this holds promise of a break from the dusty trails. People want to relax, and that can be all it takes to forget the basics. How about sending the trail assistant out every night, not just occasionally, to make sure the wagons are in a tight circle? He thought about it, and the more he did, the more it made sense to him. Yes, that's exactly what he'll do, starting tonight.

Later that morning, he stood in front of the entire group of settlers and said, "We're going to audit the wagon train every night from now on and if there's any more than 3 feet between wagons, it will be a major finding!"

He's absolutely correct. A finding would be appropriate because the circle will now be considered broken if the criterion of more than 3 feet is found between any two wagons. Now, the story goes that 2 weeks later the assistant reported back to the trail boss that he observed several wagons spaced within inches of the "3-foot rule," as it came to be called. He was right to call this condition an observation rather than a finding, because the process was still intact according to the stated criteria.

THE END OF THE JOURNEY

The auditor's journey may end with the completion of the Audit Summary; however, that report goes on ahead of the audit team for the good of the organization. Knowing how that report was received by top management closes the loop on the process for the audit team. This kind of valuable information is exactly the same as customer feedback and input, foundational elements within any of the processes they audit. The auditor's output is the Audit Summary. Top management represents the auditor's customers. It's the Act function of internal auditing. The audit was carefully planned, done, checked for thoroughness, and the Audit Summary was developed as the final act of the process.

Was the Audit Summary too long, too detailed, too short, too wordy, too filled with acronyms, too bold, uninteresting, picky, or biased? As you can see, there are many ways for the output to be less than effective, and a good audit program is as concerned with its output as any company is with its product. When possible, solicit feedback from top management. Several companies who've adopted PDCA auditing are now bringing their audit teams to top management to make the report in person. That way, both sides can directly gain understanding and respect for each other's positions and conclusions. Perhaps best of all is the opportunity to deliver the product of the auditor's journey directly to the individuals who financed and supported the trip in the first place! Given this approach, the prospect for new understanding and possible growth is an expected outcome at journey's end. The data aren't lost or forgotten—they're used to make conversation and to communicate between two important functions: communication between auditors who've just returned from examining the controls and use of company resources, and top management whose job it is to provide and look after those same resources.

Bringing together those who've checked and those whose job is to act on that information is the best possible ending of an auditor's journey. And in the language of PDCA, bringing these groups together also brings us full circle. We've carefully planned the audit using the PDCA Guide and the Audit Master. We then carried out that plan by actually doing the audit itself. We checked our findings, observations, and suggestions as we carefully developed the Audit Summary. Finally, we acted by presenting and discussing the summary with top management. Just as the PDCA cycle naturally creates opportunity for improvement, so too has the internal auditing process.

May you have many such journeys as a Process Driven Comprehensive Auditor.

Appendix A

Process Driven Comprehensive Audit

The following four-part audit report separates elements of ISO 9001:2000 into the following categories: Planning, Implementation, Evaluation, and Actions based on performance results. These four sections refer directly to Shewart and Deming's "PDCA" methodology for effective process management and are foundational to ISO 9001:2000.

Throughout this audit, sections 4.1 and 7.1 recur many times. Because 4.1 is a global planning element, while 7.1 is directed to specific processes, both are in effect at any one time within the QMS. Both also require PDCA to be effective at their respective levels and for the system of processes to work most effectively. This audit structure takes advantage of both the local and the global perspective simultaneously to create maximum value and relevance.

Development of this checklist involved placement of elements specific to this audit into their respective PDCA sections, in turn adding them to the generic 4.1 and 7.1 inquiry format provided. Therefore, all audits share a common, process driven format based on use of PDCA regardless of the process or objective under scrutiny.

Auditors are chosen so as not to audit their own work. The results of all audits are brought to the attention of top management and findings are addressed through the nonconformance process.

Part I: Plan

Audit Subject: [Enter the name of the process you're auditing]

Date:

Section 1: Motivation and Risk
(ISO 9001:2000 Sections: 5.1(c), 5.2, 5.4.2(a), 4.1(a), 4.1(d), 7.1(a))

Describe and provide evidence why [*the process you're auditing*] is important. What is the risk if it's not done properly? What would be lost or harmed?

What company quality objective(s) would be in jeopardy if [*the process you're auditing*] had a major failure?

Please give examples of why [*the process you're auditing*] is important to the organization and to its customers. Is there any evidence of these examples?

What resources are assigned to do [*the process you're auditing*]? *(computers, operating software, tools, machinery, etc.)*

Who is [*the process*] owner *(the ultimate authority)* and to whom does he/she report?

Section 2: Process Plan <u>**(Plug in PDCA Plan questions here)**</u>
(ISO 9001:2000 Sections 4.1(a), 4.1(b), 7.1(b)–7.1(d), 6.2.2(d))

Please describe how [*this process*] works in general terms.

How are the risks mentioned in the first question managed well through what you just described to me?

What other parts of the operation benefit from the success of [*the process you're auditing*]?

Can you demonstrate how the process and its performance are understood among the people who use it? Is any of this recorded in verification, validation, monitoring, and inspection records? *(Get evidence wherever possible.)*

Section 3: Key Players
(ISO 9001:2000 Sections 6.2.2, 4.1(d))

Who is/are [*the process you're auditing*] key players and to whom do they report? *(You're actually asking for a list of names for the three follow-up questions below.)*

At a later time in the audit, when you fully understand the process, interview several of the above people.

What does each person do? *(Do they have a Job Description? Get as much information as possible to use in the last question of this section.)*

Ask them if they routinely experience any obstacles or reoccurring problems. Record them here:

What records indicate that this person is competent to do the work they described to you above? *(Review competence records in the HR department. Note any big differences as observations or findings if there are no records of competence such as evaluations, certificates, training records, etc.)*

Section 4: Evaluation Method
(ISO 9001:2000 Sections 8.1, 8.2.3, 4.1(c), 4.1(e), 7.1(c), 6.2.2(d))

What measurement(s) is/are routinely used to indicate [*the process you're auditing*] performance? *(Get records!)*

How do these measurements indicate if risks described earlier are well managed? *(Get records!)*

How are these measurements related to the quality objectives of the company? *(Get records!)*

Are measurements performed at planned intervals and reported to management? *(Get records!)*

Are measurements shared with the workers [*in the department you're auditing*] for improvement? *(Get records!)*

Part II: Do

Section 1: Process Inputs
(ISO 9001:2000 Sections 4.1(b), 4.1(d), 7.5.1(a)–7.5.1(f))

What is/are the output(s) of previous process(es) that are brought to [*the process you're auditing*]? *(What serves as input to this department or function that causes them to start working on it? Get evidence wherever possible!)*

At a later time in the audit, go to the department(s) or function(s) whose output became input to this department as discovered above. Ask this department if what they send is well received, or is improvement/revision desired?

Is this input *(or material)* analyzed upon arrival to [*the process you're auditing*]? Are there records of this activity? *(Get copies or write down names, dates, PO #'s, etc., as objective proof.)*

What controls are applied to [*the process you're auditing*]? (*You're looking for work instructions, prints, budgets, etc. Remember to get evidence!)*

Are inputs received properly and well managed? *(Are there problems getting the things you need to do your job?)*

Section 2: Work Plan
(ISO 9001:2000 Sections 7.1(b), 7.5.1(a)–7.5.1(c), 8.5.1)

[In the process you're auditing]
What tools do you typically use and how are they working?

(If there are measurement tools) How and when do you use these tools? How did you know what to measure?*

Are there work instructions? *(Get evidence, if possible.)*

What improvements are anticipated if everything operates just as described?

---

*If these tools are used to measure products to determine if they meet requirements, add all section 7.6 P, D, C, and A elements.

Section 3: Process Outputs
(ISO 9001:2000 Sections 4.1(b), 7.5.2)

Is the output, or what you actually deliver, tested before [*the process you're auditing*] is completed?

Who or what receives [*the process output*] after you're done? *(Ask their input.)*

At a later time in the audit, go to the recipient(s) and ask: Is the output of [*the process you're auditing*] well received, or is improvement/revision desired?

Part III: Check

Performance
(ISO 9001:2000 Sections 4.1(e), 8.4, 8.2.1)

How is performance of [*the process you're auditing*] analyzed from the perspective of both internal and external customer satisfaction? *(Remember to get evidence for each question whenever possible!)*

How does the performance data [*of the process you're auditing*] indicate that the risks mentioned in the first question are effectively controlled? *Explain how it does.*

Do the data occasionally indicate a potential opportunity for telling others about your success or problems elsewhere in the system? Has this been done?

Are inspections and reviews proceeding as planned? Are you using the originally chosen performance criteria, or has the situation required a different approach?

How is the performance analysis you've shown to me presented to top management in a timely manner and are records available of their review/evaluation?

Part IV: Act

Improvement Plan
(ISO 9001:2000 Sections 4.1(f), 5.4.2(b), 7.1(d), 7.2.3, 8.5.1)

What evidence is available of action(s) for improvement or revision of the original plan?

Based on performance analysis, what resources were redistributed to better manage risk or to achieve the desired outcome?

What has been the customer's reaction to these revisions?

Did top management review any of these revisions before they were implemented? Did they consider (discuss or ask about) operational issues in relation to other processes in the system? Are there records of the decision to revise the process?

Part V: Supporting Audit Processes

Corrective and Preventive Action Influence
(ISO 9001:2000 Sections 8.5.2, 8.5.3)

List and briefly describe any prior nonconformance and/or corrective actions to determine effectiveness during the audit *(within the audited process)*.

List and describe any preventive actions to investigate during the audit.

Prior Audit(s) Influence
(ISO 9001:2000 Sections 5.6, 8.2.2)

How did prior audits or Management Review contribute to this audit?

Written Processes Supporting the Audit Itself:

Part VI: Audit Summary

Audit of: _____

Closing Comments, Insights and Suggestions,
Findings, and Recommendations:

General:

Observations:

Findings:

Audit Team Signatures:

_____   _____   _____

_____   _____   _____

_____   _____   _____

Opening Meeting Date: _____

Closing Meeting Date: _____

Attendees Sign-In Sheet(s) Attached

Appendix B

Quality Management Systems—Requirements

---

4 Quality management system

4.1 General requirements

The organization shall establish, document, implement, and maintain a quality management system and continually improve its effectiveness in accordance with the requirements of this International Standard.

The organization shall:

Plan   (a) Identify the processes needed for the quality management system and their application throughout the organization.

Plan   (b) Determine the sequence and interaction of these processes.

Plan   (c) Determine criteria and methods needed to ensure that both the operation and control of these processes are effective.

Do   (d) Ensure the availability of resources and information necessary to support the operation and monitoring of these processes.

Check   (e) Monitor, measure, and analyze these processes.

Act   (f) Implement actions necessary to achieve planned results and continual improvement of these processes.

These processes shall be managed by the organization in accordance with the requirements of this International Standard.

 Required Record   Documented Process   in PDCA Audit Guide

Plan, Do | Where an organization chooses to outsource any process that affects product conformity with requirements, the organization shall ensure control over such processes. Control of such outsourced processes shall be identified within the quality management system.

NOTE Processes needed for the quality management system referred to above should include processes for management activities, provisions of resources, product realization, and measurement.

4.2 Documentation requirements

4.2.1 General

The quality management system documentation shall include:

Plan, Do | (a) Documented statements of a quality policy and quality objectives

Plan, Do | (b) A quality manual

Do | (c) Documented procedures required by this International Standard

Do | (d) Documents needed by the organization to ensure the effective planning, operation, and control of its processes

Do | ✎ (e) Records required by this International Standard (see 4.2.4)

NOTE 1 Where the term "documented procedure" appears within this International Standard, this means that the procedure is established, documented, implemented, and maintained.

NOTE 2 The extent of the quality management system documentation can differ from one organization to another due to:

(a) The size of organization and type of activities

(b) The complexity of processes and their interactions

(c) The competence of personnel

NOTE 3 The documentation can be in any form or type of medium.

4.2.2 Quality manual

The organization shall establish and maintain a quality manual that includes:

Plan, Do | (a) The scope of the quality management system, including details of and justification for any exclusions

 Required Record Documented Process in PDCA Audit Guide

Plan, Do   (b) The documented procedures established for the quality management system, or reference to them

Plan, Do   (c) A description of the interaction between the processes of the quality management system

4.2.3 Control of documents

Documents required by the quality management system shall be controlled. Records are a special type of document and shall be controlled according to the requirements given in 4.2.4.

A documented procedure shall be established to define the controls needed:

Do   (a) To approve documents for adequacy prior to use

Act   (b) To review and update as necessary and reapprove documents

Check   (c) To ensure that changes and the current revision status of documents are identified

Do   (d) To ensure that relevant versions of applicable documents are available at points of use

Do   (e) To ensure that documents remain legible and readily identifiable

Do   (d) To ensure that documents of external origin are identified and their distribution controlled

Do   (g) To prevent the unintended use of obsolete documents, and to apply suitable identification to them if they are retained for any purpose

Plan, Do   ### 4.2.4 Control of records

Records shall be established and maintained to provide evidence of conformity to requirements and of the effective operation of the quality management system. Records shall remain legible, readily identifiable, and retrievable. A documented procedure shall be established to define the controls needed for the identification, storage, protection, retrieval, retention time, and disposition of records.

✎ Required Record   Documented Process   ◯   in PDCA Audit Guide

5 Management responsibility

5.1 Management commitment

Top management shall provide evidence of its commitment to the development and implementation of the quality management system and continually improving its effectiveness by:

Do

Plan, Do

Do

Check

Act

(a) Communicating to the organization the importance of meeting customer as well as statutory and regulatory requirements

(b) Establishing the quality policy

(c) Ensuring that quality objectives are established

(d) Conducting management reviews

(e) Ensuring the availability of resources

5.2 Customer focus

Plan, Do

Top management shall ensure that customer requirements are determined and are met with the aim of enhancing customer satisfaction (see 7.2.1 and 8.2.1).

5.3 Quality policy

Top management shall ensure that the quality policy:

Plan

Plan, Do

Plan, Do

Do

Check, Act

(a) Is appropriate to the purpose of this organization

(b) Includes a commitment to comply with requirements and continually improve the effectiveness of the quality management system

(c) Provides a framework for establishing and reviewing quality objectives

(d) Is communicated and understood within the organization

(e) Is reviewed for continuing suitability

5.4 Planning

5.4.1 Quality objectives

Plan, Do, Check

Top management shall ensure that quality objectives, including those needed to meet requirements for product [see 7.1(a)], are established at

 Required Record    Documented Process   in PDCA Audit Guide

relevant functions and levels within the organization. The quality objectives shall be measurable and consistent with the quality policy.

5.4.2 Quality management system planning

Top management shall ensure that:

Do (a) The planning of the quality management system is carried out in order to meet the requirements given in 4.1, as well as the quality objectives.

Act (b) The integrity of the quality management system is maintained when changes to the quality management system are planned and implemented.

5.5 Responsibility, authority, and communication

5.5.1 Responsibility and authority

Plan, Do Top management shall ensure that responsibilities and authorities are defined and communicated within the organization.

5.5.2 Management representative

Plan, Do Top management shall appoint a member of management who, irrespective of their responsibilities, shall have responsibility and authority that includes:

Do (a) Ensuring that processes needed for the quality management system are established, implemented, and maintained

Do (b) Reporting to top management on the performance of the quality management system and any need for improvement

Do, Act (c) Ensuring the promotion of awareness of customer requirements throughout the organization

NOTE The responsibility of a management representative can include liaison with external parties on matters relating to the quality management system.

 Required Record 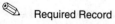 Documented Process in PDCA Audit Guide

5.5.3 Internal communication

Do

Top management shall ensure that appropriate communication processes are established within the organization and that communication takes place regarding the effectiveness of the quality management system.

5.6 Management review

5.6.1 General

Check

Top management shall review the organization's quality management system, at planned intervals, to ensure its continuing suitability, adequacy, and effectiveness. This review shall include assessing opportunities for improvement and the need for changes to the quality management system, including the quality policy and quality objectives.

Do

✎ Records from management reviews shall be maintained (see 4.2.4).

5.6.2 Review input

The input to management review shall include information on:

Check	(a) Results of audits
Check	(b) Customer feedback
Check	(c) Process performance and product conformity
Check	(d) Status of preventive and corrective actions
Do, Act	(e) Follow-up actions from previous management reviews
Plan	(f) Changes that could affect the quality management system
Do,	(g) Recommendations for improvement

5.6.3 Review output

The output from the management review shall include any decisions and actions related to:

 Required Record   Documented Process   in PDCA Audit Guide

Act	(a) Improvement of the effectiveness of the quality management system and its processes
Act	(b) Improvement of product related to customer requirements
Act	(c) Resource needs

6 Resource management

6.1 Provision of resources

The organization shall determine and provide the resources needed:

Do	(a) To implement and maintain the quality management system and continually improve its effectiveness
Do	(b) To enhance customer satisfaction by meeting customer requirements

6.2 Human resources

6.2.1 General

Plan	Personnel performing work affecting product quality shall be competent on the basis of appropriate education, training, skills and experience.

Plan	**6.2.2 Competence, awareness, and training**

The organization shall:

Plan	(a) Determine the necessary competence for personnel performing work affecting product quality.
Do	(b) Provide training or take other actions to satisfy these needs.
Check	(c) Evaluate the effectiveness of the actions taken.
Act	(d) Ensure that its personnel are aware of the relevance and importance of their activities and how they contribute to the achievement of the quality objectives.
Do	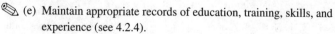 (e) Maintain appropriate records of education, training, skills, and experience (see 4.2.4).

 Required Record   Documented Process   in PDCA Audit Guide

6.3 Infrastructure

The organization shall determine, provide, and maintain the infrastructure needed to achieve conformity to product requirements. Infrastructure includes, as applicable:

Plan, Do (a) Buildings, workspace, and associated utilities

Plan, Do (b) Process equipment (both hardware and software)

Plan, Do (c) Supporting services (such as transport or communication)

6.4 Work environment

Plan, Do The organization shall determine and manage the work environment needed to achieve conformity to product requirements.

7 Product realization

7.1 Planning of product realization

The organization shall plan and develop the processes needed for product realization. Planning of product realization shall be consistent with the requirements of the other processes of the quality management system (see 4.1).

In planning product realization, the organization shall determine the following, as appropriate:

Plan (a) Quality objectives and requirements for the product

Plan, Do (b) The need to establish processes, documents, and provide resources specific to the product

Plan, Do, Check (c) Required verification, validation, monitoring, inspection, and test activities specific to the product and the criteria for product acceptance

Do (d) Records needed to provide evidence that the realization processes and resulting product meet requirements (see 4.2.4)

The output of this planning shall be in a form suitable for the organization's methods of operations.

NOTE 1 A document specifying the processes of the quality management system (including the product realization processes) and

 Required Record   Documented Process   in PDCA Audit Guide

the resources to be applied to a specific product, project, or contract can be referred to as a "quality plan."

NOTE 2 The organization may also apply the requirements given in 7.3 to the development of product realization processes.

7.2 Customer-related processes

7.2.1 Determination of requirements related to the product

The organization shall determine:

Plan (a) Requirements specified by the customer, including the requirements for delivery and post-delivery activities

Plan (b) Requirements not stated by the customer but necessary for specified or intended use, where known

Plan (c) Statutory and regulatory requirements related to the product

Plan (d) Any additional requirements determined by the organization

7.2.2 Review of requirements related to the product

Do The organization shall review the requirements related to the product. This review shall be conducted prior to the organizations commitment to supply a product to the customer (for example, submission of tenders, acceptance of contracts on orders, acceptance of changes to contracts or orders) and shall ensure that:

Do (a) Product requirements are defined.

Do (b) Contract or order requirements differing from those previously expressed are received.

Check (c) Its organization has the ability to meet the defined requirements.

Do ✎ Records of the results of the review and actions arising from the review shall be maintained (see 4.2.4).

Do Where the customer provides no documented statement of requirement, the customer requirements shall be confirmed by the organization before acceptance.

Act Where product requirements are changed, the organization shall ensure that relevant documents are amended and that relevant personnel are made aware of the changed requirements.

 Required Record   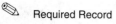 **Documented Process**   **in PDCA Audit Guide**

NOTE In some situations, such as Internet sales, a formal review is impractical for each order. Instead, the review can cover relevant product information such as catalogues or advertising material.

7.2.3 Customer communication

The organization shall determine and implement effective arrangements for communicating with customers in relation to:

Do   (a) Product information

Do   (b) Inquiries, contracts on order handling, including amendments

Do   (c) Customer feedback, including customer complaints

7.3 Design and development

7.3.1 Design and development planning

The organization shall plan and control the design and development of product.

During the design and development planning, the organization shall determine:

Plan, Do (a) The design and development stages

Check   (b) The review, verification, and validation that are appropriate to each design and development stage

Plan, Do (c) The responsibilities and authorities for design and development

Plan, Do The organization shall manage the interfaces between different groups involved in design and development to ensure effective communication and clear assignment of responsibility.

Act   Planning output shall be updated, as appropriate, as the design and development progresses.

7.3.2 Design and development inputs

Do   ✎ Inputs relating to product requirements shall be determined and records maintained (see 4.2.4).

 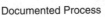

These inputs shall include:

Plan, Do   (a) Functional and performance requirements

Plan, Do   (b) Applicable statutory and regulatory requirements

Plan, Do   (c) Where applicable, information derived from previous similar designs

Plan, Do   (d) Other requirements essential for design and development

---

7.3.3   Design and development outputs

The outputs of design and development shall be provided in a form that enables verification against the design and development input and shall be approved prior to release.

Design and development outputs shall:

Check, Act   (a) Meet the input requirements for design and development.

Check, Act   (b) Provide appropriate information for purchasing, production, and service provision.

Check, Act   (c) Contain or reference product acceptance criteria.

Check, Act   (d) Specify the characteristics of the product that are essential for its safe and proper use.

7.3.4   Design and development review

At suitable stages, systematic reviews of design and development shall be performed in accordance with planned arrangements (see 7.3.1):

Check   (a) To evaluate the ability of the results of design and development to meet requirements

Act   (b) To identify any problems and propose necessary actions

Do   Participants in such reviews shall include representatives of functions concerned with the design and development stage(s) being reviewed.

Do   Records of the results of the reviews and any necessary actions shall be maintained (see 4.2.4).

   Required Record   Documented Process   ◯   in PDCA Audit Guide

7.3.5 Design and development verification

Check

Verification shall be performed in accordance with planned arrangements (see 7.3.1) to ensure that the design and development outputs have met the design and development input requirements.

Do

 Records of the results of the verification and any necessary actions shall be maintained (see 4.2.4).

7.3.6 Design and development validation

Check

Act

Design and development validation shall be performed in accordance with planned arrangements (see 7.3.1) to ensure that the resulting product is capable of meeting the requirements for specified application or intended use, where known. Wherever practicable, validation shall be completed prior to the delivery or implementation of the product.

Do

 Records of the results of validation and any necessary actions shall be maintained (see 4.2.4).

7.3.7 Control of design and development changes

Check

Act

Design and development changes shall be identified and records maintained. The changes shall be reviewed, verified, and validated, as appropriate, and approved before implementation. The review of design and development changes shall include evaluation of the effect of the changes on constituent parts and product already delivered.

Do

 Records of the results of the review of changes and any necessary actions shall be maintained (see 4.2.4).

7.4 Purchasing

7.4.1 Purchasing process

Check

The organization shall ensure that purchased product conforms to specified purchase requirements. The type and extent of control applied to the supplier and the purchased product shall be dependent upon the effect of the purchased product on subsequent product realization or the final product.

 Required Record   Documented Process   in PDCA Audit Guide

Do | The organization shall evaluate and select suppliers based on their ability to supply product in accordance with the organization's requirements. Criteria for selection, evaluation, and reevaluation shall be established.

Do | Records of the results of evaluations and any necessary actions arising from the evaluation shall be maintained (see 4.2.4).

7.4.2 Purchasing information

Purchasing information shall describe the product to be purchased, including, where appropriate:

Plan | (a) Requirements for approval of product, procedures, processes, and equipment

Plan | (b) Requirements for qualification of personnel

Plan | (c) Quality management system requirements

Plan, Do | The organization shall ensure the adequacy of specified purchase requirements prior to their communication to the supplier.

7.4.3 Verification of purchased product

Check, Act | The organization shall establish and implement the inspection or other activities necessary for ensuring that purchased product meets specified purchase requirements.

Do | Where the organization or its customer intends to perform verification at the supplier's premises, the organization shall state the intended verification arrangements and method of product release in the purchasing information.

7.5 Production and service provision

(7.5.1) Control of production and service provision

The organization shall plan and carry out production and service provision under controlled conditions. Controlled conditions shall include, as applicable:

 Required Record  Documented Process in PDCA Audit Guide

Do	(a) The availability of information that describes the characteristics of the product
Do	(b) The availability of work instructions, as necessary
Do	(c) The use of suitable equipment
Do	(d) The availability and use of monitoring and measurement devices
Do	(e) The implementation of monitoring and measurement
Do	(f) The implementation of release, delivery, and post-delivery activities

7.5.2 Validation of processes for production and service provision

Do   The organization shall validate any processes for production and service provision where the resulting output cannot be verified by subsequent monitoring or measurement. This includes any processes where deficiencies become apparent only after the product is in use or the service has been delivered.

Check   Validation shall demonstrate the ability of these processes to achieve planned results.

The organization shall establish arrangements for these processes including, as applicable:

Do   (a) Defined criteria for review and approval of the processes

Do   (b) Approval of equipment and qualifications of personnel

Do   (c) Use of specific methods and procedures

Do   ✎ (d) Requirements for records (see 4.2.4)

Check, Act   (e) Revalidation

7.5.3 Identification and traceability

Do   Where appropriate, the organization shall identify the product by suitable means throughout product realization.

Do   The organization shall identify the product status with respect to monitoring and measurement requirements.

Do   ✎ Where traceability is a requirement, the organization shall control and record the unique identification of the product (see 4.2.4).

NOTE In some industry sectors, configuration management is a means by which identification and traceability are maintained.

 Required Record   Documented Process   in PDCA Audit Guide

7.5.4 Customer property

Do

The organization shall exercise care with customer property while it is under the organization's control or being used by the organization. The organization shall identify, verify, protect, and safeguard customer property provided for use or incorporation into the product.

Do

 If any customer property is lost, damaged, or otherwise found to be unsuitable for use, this shall be reported to the customer and records maintained (see 4.2.4).

NOTE Customer property can include intellectual property.

7.5.5 Preservation of product

Do

The organization shall preserve the conformity of product during internal processing and delivery to the intended destination. This preservation shall include identification, handling, packaging, storage, and protection. Preservation shall also apply to the constituent parts of a product.

7.6 Control of monitoring and measuring devices

Plan

The organization shall determine the monitoring and measurement to be undertaken and the monitoring and measuring devices needed to provide evidence of conformity of product to determined requirements (see 7.2.1).

Do

The organization shall establish processes to ensure that monitoring and measurement can be carried out and are carried out in a manner that is consistent with the monitoring and measurement requirements.

Where necessary to ensure valid results, measuring equipment shall:

Do

(a) Be calibrated or verified at specified intervals, or prior to use, against measurement standards traceable to international or national measurement standards; where no such standards exist,

Check, Act

the basis used for calibration or verification shall be recorded

(b) Be adjusted or readjusted as necessary

Do

(c) Be identified to enable the calibration status to be determined

 Required Record  Documented Process in PDCA Audit Guide

Do	(d) Be safeguarded from adjustments that would invalidate the measurement result
Do	(e) Be protected from damage and deterioration during handling, maintenance, and storage
Check	In addition, the organization shall assess and record the validity of the previous measuring results when the equipment is found not to conform to requirements.
Do	✎ The organization shall take appropriate action on the equipment and any product affected. Records of the results of calibration and verification shall be maintained (see 4.2.4).
Check, Act	When used in the monitoring and measurement of specified requirements the ability of computer software to satisfy the intended application shall be confirmed. This shall be undertaken prior to initial use and reconfirmed as necessary.
	NOTE See ISO 10012-1 and ISO 10012-2 for guidance.

8 Measurement, analysis, and improvement

Plan, Do, Check, Act

8.1 General

The organization shall plan and implement the monitoring, measurement, analysis, and improvement processes needed:

Act	(a) To demonstrate conformity of the product
Act	(b) To ensure conformity of the quality management system
Act	(c) To continually improve the effectiveness of the quality management system

This shall include determination of applicable methods, including statistical techniques, and the extent of use.

8.2 Monitoring and measurements

8.2.1 Customer satisfaction

Do, Check	As one of the measurements of the performance of the quality management system, the organization shall monitor information relating to customer perception as to whether the organization has met

 Required Record Documented Process in PDCA Audit Guide

customer requirements. The methods for obtaining and using this information shall be determined.

8.2.2 Internal audit

The organization shall conduct internal audits at planned intervals to determine whether the quality management system:

Check   (a) Conforms to the planned arrangements (see 7.1), to the requirements of this International Standard, and to the quality management system requirements established by the organization

Check   (b) Is effectively implemented and maintained

Plan, Do   An audit program shall be planned, taking into consideration the status and importance of the processes and areas to be audited, as well as the results of previous audits. The audit criteria, scope, frequency, and methods shall be defined. Selection of auditors and conduct of audits shall ensure objectivity and impartiality of the audit process. Auditors shall not audit their own work.

Do   ✎ The responsibility and requirements for planning and conducting audits, and for reporting results and maintaining records (see 4.2.4) shall be defined in a documented procedure.

Act   The management responsible for the area being audited shall ensure that actions are taken without undue delay to eliminate detected nonconformities and their causes. Follow-up activities shall include the verification of the actions taken and the reporting of verification results (see 8.5.2).

NOTE See ISO 10011-1, ISO 10011-2, and ISO 10011-3 for guidance.

8.2.3 Monitoring and measurement of processes

Check,   The organization shall apply suitable methods for monitoring and,
Act   where applicable, measurement of the quality management system processes. These methods shall demonstrate the ability of the processes to achieve planned results. When planned results are not achieved, correction and corrective action shall be taken, as appropriate, to ensure conformity of the product.

 Required Record   Documented Process   in PDCA Audit Guide

8.2.4 Monitoring and measurement of product

Do

Check

The organization shall monitor and measure the characteristics of the product to verify that the product requirements have been met. This shall be carried out at appropriate states of the product realization process in accordance with the planned arrangements (see 7.1).

Do

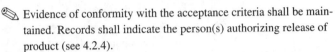 Evidence of conformity with the acceptance criteria shall be maintained. Records shall indicate the person(s) authorizing release of product (see 4.2.4).

Act

Product release and service delivery shall not proceed until the planned arrangements (see 7.1) have been satisfactorily completed, unless otherwise approved by a relevant authority and, where applicable, by the customer.

8.3 Control of nonconforming product

Do

The organization shall ensure that product that does not conform to product requirements is identified and controlled to prevent its unintended use or delivery. The controls and related responsibilities and authorities for dealing with nonconformity product shall be defined in a documented procedure.

The organization shall deal with nonconforming product by one or more of the following ways:

Do

(a) By taking action to eliminate the detected nonconformity

Do

(b) By authorizing its use, release, or acceptance under concession by a relevant authority and, where applicable, by the customer

Act

(c) By taking action to preclude its original intended use or application

Do

Records of the nature of nonconformities and any subsequent actions taken, including concessions obtained, shall be maintained (see 4.2.4).

Check, Act

When nonconforming product is corrected it shall be subject to reverification to demonstrate conformity to the requirements.

Check, Act

When nonconforming product is detected after delivery or use has started, the organization shall take action appropriate to the effectiveness or potential effects of the nonconformity.

 Required Record    Documented Process   in PDCA Audit Guide

8.4 Analysis of data

**Do,
Check**

The organization shall determine, collect, and analyze appropriate data to demonstrate suitability and effectiveness of the quality management system and to evaluate where continual improvement of the effectiveness of the quality management system can be made. This shall include data generated as a result of monitoring and measurement and from other relevant sources.

**Do,
Check**

The analysis of data shall provide information relating to:

**Do,
Check**

(a) Customer satisfaction (see 8.2.1)

(b) Conformity to product requirements (see 7.2.1)

**Do,
Check**

(c) Characteristics and trends of processes and products including opportunities for preventive action

**Do,
Check**

(d) Suppliers

8.5 Improvement

8.5.1 Continual improvement

Act

The organization shall continually improve the effectiveness of the quality management system through the use of the quality policy, quality objectives, audit results, analysis of data, corrective and preventive actions, and management review.

8.5.2 Corrective action

Act

The organization shall take action to eliminate the cause of nonconformities in order to prevent recurrence. Corrective actions shall be appropriate to the effects of the nonconformities encountered.

A documented procedure shall be established to define requirements for:

Plan

(a) Reviewing nonconformities (including customer complaints)

Check

(b) Determining the causes of nonconformities

Plan

(c) Evaluating the need for action to ensure that nonconformities do not recur

 Required Record   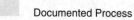 Documented Process   in PDCA Audit Guide

Act	(d) Determining and implementing action needed
Do	(e) Records of the results of action taken (see 4.2.4)
Act	(f) Reviewing corrective action taken

(8.5.3) Preventive action

The organization shall determine action to eliminate the causes of potential nonconformities in order to prevent their occurrence. Preventive actions shall be appropriate to the effects of the potential problems.

A documented procedure shall be established to define requirements for:

Act	(a) Determining potential nonconformities and their causes
Plan	(b) Evaluating the need for action to prevent occurrence of nonconformities
Check,	(c) Determining and implementing action needed
Act	(d) Records of results of action taken (see 4.2.4)
Act	(e) Reviewing preventive action taken

 Required Record   Documented Process ◯ in PDCA Audit Guide

Appendix C
Sample Audit

The following sample audit was developed to demonstrate the PDCA approach and its outcome. In the following audit, an observation was reported to top management that not all purchase orders are managed as described in work instructions and process control documents within the Purchasing department. The situation was not considered a finding, as the issue was found to be more of appearance than an actual break in the process. However, the audit team did recommend that process documentation be updated to include individual releases of contract and blanket purchase orders.

You will notice that a table or spreadsheet system was employed for multiple evidence sampling where each process required the same sort of information to be recorded. It's a good method for quickly entering the yes/no status of each component you're expecting to find in each sample. Auditors often find themselves overwhelmed by the amount of detail they must record during the audit. This is one of several methods to capture repeated entries of information similar to each sample.

Sample quantity is always a concern. There are many who insist on six to eight samples of each record. Others are of the mind to check several and dig deeper only if anomalies are found as they investigate. Still others employ a more scientific approach and insist on specific sample quantities, determined statistically, based on the total number of reports, forms, or records they are investigating. Choose whatever approach makes the most sense to you and stick with it. Make that choice based on value and the return on the investment in time that all these checks require. If you choose too few, sooner or later the results of a thin scan will make themselves known. If you choose too many, the audit becomes an exercise in compliance to format, rather than an examination of process effectiveness. Revise when necessary along with the benefit of experience to guide the improvement.

In this audit, an entry in bold type represents a copied record (not included) that was later attached to the Audit Master as evidence. Suppliers' names, dates, and quantities are fictitious. And to everyone at Northern Pipe Products, Inc. of Fargo, North Dakota, thank you for serving as audit subjects and for openly sharing this information.

Please remember that the degree of detail, questioning technique, and writing style are subject to each individual auditor's skills, attitude, and experience. Some audits might appear quite similar to this example, others might be much simpler, and others might be far more complex. But if you use the Audit Master to direct the flow of events, the depth of your first audit will be just as comprehensive as your hundredth.

Process Driven Comprehensive Audit

The following four-part audit report separates elements of ISO 9001:2000 into the following categories: Planning, Implementation, Evaluation, and Actions based on performance results. These four sections refer directly to Deming's "PDCA" methodology for effective process management and are foundational to ISO 9001:2000.

Throughout this audit, sections 4.1 and 7.1 recur many times. Because 4.1 is a global planning element, while 7.1 is directed to specific processes, both are in effect at any one time within the QMS. Both also require PDCA to be effective at their respective levels and for the system of processes to work most effectively. This audit structure takes advantage of both the local and the global perspective simultaneously to create maximum value and relevance.

Development of this checklist involved placement of elements specific to this audit into their respective PDCA sections, in turn adding them to the generic 4.1 and 7.1 inquiry format provided. Therefore, all audits share a common, process driven format based on use of PDCA regardless of the process or objective under scrutiny.

Auditors are chosen so as not to audit their own work. The results of all audits are brought to the attention of top management and findings are addressed through the nonconformance process.

Part I: Plan

Audit Subject: <u>Purchasing</u>
June 23–24, 2004

Section 1: Motivation and Risk
(ISO 9001:2000 Sections: 5.1(c), 5.2, 5.4.2(a), 4.1(a), 4.1(d), 7.1(a))

Describe and provide evidence why Purchasing is important. What is the risk if it's not done properly? What would be lost or harmed?

Interviewed J Martens: Risks would be over-pay of materials. We would have production interruptions. We would not be profitable.

What company quality objective(s) would be in jeopardy if Purchasing had a major failure?

Interviewed J Martens: Reduced Cost of Quality and Customer Satisfaction.

Please give examples of why Purchasing is important to the organization and to its customers. Is there any evidence of these examples?

*Interviewed J Martens: Resin contracts **XYZ Material 2002, 2003, and 2004 Resin Contract.** Contracts indicate high degree of control of price annually. Contract per pound expense indicates no spikes or major increases = stability, control, strong relationship with supplier. **2002, 2003, and 2004 Annual Quality Review** indicates XYZ Material to be one of NPP's key, or critical suppliers. Report card grade consistently above average for criteria: price, delivery, service, and quality.*

Customers: J Martens explained that if resin prices were higher, sales would be severely impacted, as this is a *commodity-based business.* What resources are assigned to do Purchasing? *(computers, operating software, tools, machinery, etc.)*

Interviewed J Martens: Visual operating software, NPP computer network, Keith Lindsey and Purchasing staff of 2, Parts room and warehouse, Parts truck.

Who is the Purchasing Process owner *(the ultimate authority)* and to whom does he/she report?

Interviewed J Martens: I am the owner and I report to Wayne Voorhees, President.

Section 2: Process Plan
(ISO 9001:2000 Sections 4.1(a), 4.1(b), 7.1(b), 7.1(c), 7.1(d), 6.2.2(d))

Please describe how Purchasing works in general terms.

Interviewed J Martens: There is a formal purchasing process, but in general, a person or department requests that something be bought and that requisition comes to Keith or me for processing. Appropriate vendor is investigated and chosen, purchase order is produced, material is ordered, upon receipt, material is inspected and placed in stores. Material is green-tagged, if approved. (Martens claims all incoming material is tagged with green acceptance sticker–investigate later.)

Are the risks mentioned in the first question managed well through what was just described to me?

Risks appear to be well managed from reports received and evidence collected: **<u>Monthly Purchasing Reports for January through June, 2004</u>**–*Reports indicate 24-hour turn-around of requisitions and no late deliveries.*

What other parts of the operation benefit from the success of Purchasing?

Interviewed J Martens: Virtually all departments do, but especially Production. Production relies on certain materials to produce pipe in the expected manner. XYZ Material is known to have certain extrusion characteristics that are preferred by Production. (Investigate Production's desire to use XYZ Material.) Sales department also benefits because Purchasing can react quickly to new sales demands. Speed of processing requisitions is only one part of the Purchasing process ability to react quickly. A strong key supplier base is essential to maintain our flexibility.

Can you demonstrate how the process and its performance are understood among the people who use it? Is any of this recorded in verification, validation, monitoring, and inspection records? *(Get evidence wherever possible.)*

Interviewed J Martens: **Monthly Purchasing Reports for January through June, 2004**—*This report is produced by Keith Lindsey, Purchasing Agent, and delivered by Lindsey at Monthly Quality Council/ Manager's Meetings. (Check with Keith Lindsey to verify that he does these things.)*

7.4.2 Requirements for product approval include–(product, procedure, processes, equipment):
Interviewed J Martens:
a. *Requisition dollar amount maximums, purchasing procedure **ISO Document PURC_100.doc Rev C – Purchasing Process**, previously mentioned resources = equipment.*
b. *Personnel are qualified according to job descriptions and required training found in Education Coordinator's office. J Martens and K Lindsey (investigate to determine if records are available to prove competence as required in ISO 9001:2000 Section 6.2.2).*
c. *Quality Management System requirements: J Martens: The QMS requires that Purchasing deliver a monthly report, that the Purchasing manager attends weekly Quality Council Meetings, that vendors are graded and improvement is expected, etc.*

Section 3: Key Players
(ISO 9001:2000 Sections 6.2.2, 4.1(d))

Who is/are Purchasing key players and to whom do they report?
*(You're actually asking for a list of names for the three follow-up
questions below.)*

J. Martens, K. Lindsey

<u>At a later time in the audit, when you fully understand the process,
interview several of the above people.</u>

What does each person do? *(Do they have a Job Description? Get as
much information as possible to use in the last question of this
section.)*

*Interviewed Kristin Munro, Education Coordinator: Jeff Martens is the
VP of Purchasing and Keith Lindsay's title is Purchasing Agent. Their
job descriptions appear to match their observed activities. Jeff and
Keith both have job descriptions, located in the HR directory on the
NPP network.*

Ask them if they routinely experience any obstacles or reoccurring
problems. Record them here:

*Interviewed J Martens: Getting information from Sales department in a
timely manner. Working with all the issues from each division and
department to keep everyone happy. Resin prices are impossible to
predict–constantly fluctuating.*

*Interviewed K Lindsey: Number one problem is parts taken from the
Part Room and not properly signed out. Finding reliable shippers in
emergency situations. Processing multiple requisitions that could have
been combined into one.*

What records indicate that this person is competent to do the work they
described to you above? *(Review competence records in the HR
department. Note any big differences as Observations or Findings if
there are no records of competence such as evaluations, certificates,
training records, etc.)*

Interviewed K Munro: Job descriptions and evaluations indicate skills, education, and experience minimums as well as training required and reviewed every 6 months. Both Jeff and Keith received evaluation overall grades of 3 or above (on a scale of 1–5). This indicates competence according to NPP HR process documentation.

Section 4: Evaluation Method
(ISO 9001:2000 Sections 8.1, 8.2.3, 4.1(c), 4.1(e), 7.1(c), 6.2.2(d))

What measurement(s) is/are routinely used to indicate Purchasing performance? *(Get records!)*

Interviewed J Martens: **Monthly Purchasing Reports** *provide ongoing performance information to Top Management.* **Annual Quality Review** *summarizes Purchasing performance and supplier performance. Measurements include percent of on-time delivery, days to order fulfillment. Vendors are rated on a scale of 1–5 using previously described criteria. Unable to "measure" resin prices; however, they are carefully monitored throughout the year.*

How do these measurements indicate if risks described earlier are well managed? *(Get records!)*

Interviewed J Martens: Risk (Production impact): "Annual Quality Review" indicates no lost production hours due to material shortages. Overpayment of materials: **2002 and 2003 Financial Statements (Purchasing Section only)** *provided by Jeff indicates Purchasing Department to have been under budget for both years. This includes all estimated prices for purchased materials. Profitability: Both years showed a profit that would not have been possible with Purchasing mismanagement (verify profitability with CFO at a later time).*

How are these measurements related to the quality objectives of the company? *(Get records!)*

Objectives: Customer Satisfaction and Reduced Cost of Quality are directly affected by the success or failure of the Purchasing process, as shown by all evidence thus far collected. **2004 Cost or Quality Reports (monthly)**

Are measurements performed at planned intervals and reported to management? (Get records!)

Interviewed J Martens: Yes, as indicated above–weekly, monthly, and annual reports. **Monthly Purchasing Reports**

Are measurements shared with the Purchasing workers for improvement? *(Get records!)*

Interviewed J Martens: Records are obviously shared, because Keith generates the reports!

Part II: Do

Section 1: Process Inputs
(ISO 9001:2000 Sections 4.1(b), 4.1(d), 7.5.1(a)–7.5.1(f))

What is/are the output(s) of previous process(es) that are brought to Purchasing? *(What serves as input to this department or function that causes them to start working on it? Get evidence wherever possible!)*

Interviewed J Martens: Sales brings its orders to my attention, which, in turn, are discussed at Scheduling Meetings. Normally, orders are placed 6 weeks in advance (this makes it difficult to be as flexible as I would like).

Input is also received from the Maintenance department. Most purchase requests are maintenance-related. The MP2 system manages the bulk of these orders.

At a later time in the audit, go to the department(s) or function(s) whose output became input to this department as discovered above. Ask this department if what they send is well received, or is improvement/revision desired?

Interviewed Warren Etches, VP Sales and Marketing: Confirmed that he and his department provide Purchasing with upcoming order information and stated that there are few, if any, problems within the normal course of events. He stated that his output (Sales orders and revised schedules) is generally well received with occasional problems when a rush order is placed. However, this is to be expected.

Interviewed Randy Kennedy, Maintenance Manager: Says that he works closely with Keith Lindsey (shares the same office as Keith) and that while there were initial transition issues concerning MP2, today things are flowing smoothly.

Is this input *(or material)* analyzed upon arrival to Purchasing? Are there records of this activity? *(Get copies or write down names, dates, PO #'s, etc., as objective proof.)*

*Interviewed J Martens: Sales upcoming orders are brought to my attention as they come in and my job is to compare material quantities on order with the expected demand. Martens says he uses the **Railcar***

Tracking Form *to place and monitor all resin shipments from key suppliers.*

Customer Sales Order # 09987 *dated Jan 15, 2004. Reviewed Jan 15, 2004.* **_Resin Purchase Order # 7822104_** *placed Jan 16, 2004.*

Wood Purchase Order # 234471-10 *placed Jan 16, 2004 (Sideboards for pallets). Review dates noted by initials on tracking form and purchase orders. (Check with Paul Tupa, Inventory Control, to verify that Customer Sales Order #09987 was shipped on time.)*

What controls are applied to Purchasing?

Interviewed J Martens: Many have been noted thus far in this audit. They include budget, annual contracts, vendor criteria (also based on product offerings as a control), QMS itself, receiving inspection, stated requisition maximum amounts per positions of authority.

Are inputs received properly and well managed? *(Are there problems getting the things you need to do your job?)*

Interviewed J Martens: There were no reported incidents, other than "hot orders."

Section 2: Work Plan
(ISO 9001:2000 Sections 7.1(b), 7.5.1(a)–7.5.1(c), 8.5.1)

In Purchasing, what tools do you typically use and how are they working?

Interviewed J Martens: MP2, Visual, calibrated tape measures and micrometers. They are working as planned.

Are there work instructions? *(Get evidence, if possible.)*

*Interviewed J Martens: **Purchasing Work Instructions** are available online for all Purchasing activities in compliance with ISO 9001:2000 and Sarbanes-Oxley legislation.*

What improvements are anticipated if everything operates just as described?

Interviewed J Martens: Vendor corrective actions and vendor report cards are expected to produce improvement in vendor performance annually.

7.4.1 Purchasing Process

Interviewed J Martens: Selection of suppliers is based on one of two methods:

*1. evidence of **Registration to ISO 9001:2000**,*

*2. successfully pass a **Supplier Audit** (this includes transportation companies as well).*

Key Vendor	*Registered to 9001:2000*	*Successful Audit*
Vendor XYZ	*x*	
Vendor ABC		*x*
Vendor 123		*x*
Vendor 890	x	

Cover sheets for Audits and ISO Registration are attached to this report.

Criteria already defined as price, delivery, quality, and service. **Evaluations** already mentioned previously in this audit are contained in past year's "Annual Quality Review." Each year's average total scores show overall improvement from one year to the next.

Section 3: Process Outputs
(ISO 9001:2000 Sections 4.1(b), 7.5.2)

Is the output, or what you actually deliver, tested before Purchasing is completed?

Interviewed J Martens: Incoming Inspection is performed when ordered goods are received. Orders that pass inspection are issued green pass stickers, indicating that they are ready for use.

Material	*Pass Sticker Present?*	*PO Visible?*	*Inspected By*	*Date*
C-900 12" Gaskets	x	x	KL	March 3, 2004
8" Sewer Gaskets	x	x	KL	April 21, 2004
34.5" wood side boards	x	x	DF	April 16, 2004
3/4 inch banding	x	x	KL	June 9, 2004

Who or what receives Purchasing activities after you're done? *(Ask their input.)*

Interviewed J Martens: Production and Maintenance.

At a later time in the audit, go to the recipient(s) and ask: Is the output of Purchasing well-received, or is improvement/revision desired?

See previous interviews.

Part III: Check

Performance
(ISO 9001:2000 Sections 4.1(e), 8.4, 8.2.1)

Is performance of Purchasing analyzed from the perspective of both internal and external customer satisfaction? *(Remember to get evidence for each question whenever possible!)*

*Interviewed J Martens: Internal customers (Employees) are surveyed annually. There have been no reports of Purchasing representing a negative influence through its work. Audit team checked **2002 and 2003 Employee Satisfaction Surveys** and found no Purchasing issues noted.*

*Interviewed P Tupa, Inventory Control: Order #09987 due to Ajax Water Works Company June 27, 2004. Shipped June 26, 2004, with **Bill of Lading # 97258** dated June 26, 2004.*

7.4.1 Ensuring that purchased product conforms to specified requirements

Interviewed J Martens: All incoming material goes through the Purchase Order process. We only order things that have been clearly defined, first on the Requisition Form, secondly on the Purchase Order itself. Many times, Keith is ordering something from a catalogue and the catalogue item number defines the specifics of the desired item. Overall, the amount of detail on the Purchase Order depends on the complexity of the order.

Purchase Order #	Item Description	Complete Description?	Approvals Noted?
#1009987	Prime Resin	Yes	No
#652287	Extruder Control Panel	Yes!!!!	Yes
#2587754	Office Supplies– General Supplies	Yes	No
#644275	Wax (micro ingredient)	CAT #	Yes

(After noting missing approvals above, six other PO's were subsequently reviewed from the past 6 months. All were found to be "complete.")

OBSERVATION: *Lack of authorizations on 2 of the 4 Purchase Order line items were explained by Keith Lindsey as standard operating procedure. Prime Resin, as a railcar item, is covered by a blanket purchase order with full description when the contract is signed. From*

that point on, it's considered a "re-order." Office Supplies are loosely managed, where anyone can enter item descriptions when we run out of that item. All office supplies are supplied by one contractor, who also has an agreement with us to replenish the supply room using this system.

Do the Purchasing performance data indicate that the risks mentioned in the first question are effectively controlled?

Auditors believe that, given all evidence collected and interviews performed, Purchasing has controlled all risks mentioned.

Do the data indicate a potential opportunity for telling others about your success or problems elsewhere in the system? Has this been done?

*Interviewed J Martens: All purchasing data are shared with everyone in the company through **Quality Council** and **Monthly Managers' Meetings**. **Open Book Management Meetings** are also used to tell others the current status of the Purchasing process. Anyone in any of these meetings should see that it doesn't matter where the Requisition Order comes from, I treat it the same. Since all this is done in the open, anyone can suggest an improvement if they think of it! **Meeting minutes for May 2004 are attached to this report.***

Are inspections and reviews proceeding as planned? Are you using the originally chosen performance criteria, or has the situation required a different approach?

Interviewed J Martens: Incoming inspections and supplier reviews have not changed since we started using them in 1999. Performance criteria also are the same since 1999.

Is the performance analysis you've shown to me presented to top management in a timely manner and are records available of their review/evaluation?

Interviewed J Martens: As stated earlier in this audit, all reports and results are shared at weekly and monthly meetings.

Part IV: Act

Improvement Plan
(ISO 9001:2000 Sections 4.1(f), 5.4.2(b), 7.1(d), 7.2.3, 8.5.1)

What evidence is available of action(s) for improvement or revision of the original Purchasing plan?

Interviewed J Martens: Visual operating software was upgraded last year and in the process, streamlined the Purchasing process by linking the Railcar Tracking Form with Inventory Management within Visual. We added Sarbanes-Oxley specifics in Q2 2004, which further controls and defines Purchasing from a financial point of view.

Based on performance analysis, what resources were redistributed to better manage risk or to achieve the desired outcome?

Interviewed J Martens: None. No changes were made based on performance analysis. We can see that things are just getting better.

What has been the customer's reaction to these revisions?

Interviewed J Martens: The "Annual Quality Review 2002 and 2003–Sales Survey" shows no delivery issues. Therefore, no material availability issues.

Did top management review any of these revisions before they were implemented? Did they consider (discuss or ask about) operational issues in relation to other processes in the system? Are there records of the decision to revise the process?

*Interviewed J Martens: All revisions for all operations and process changes are reviewed and/or approved by the Quality Council (top management at NPP). **Process Change Notice for Sarbanes-Oxley Process additions, approved by Quality Council on 03/15/04, is attached.***

7.4.3 Verification of Purchased Product

Interviewed J Martens: We've already discussed this several times in this audit.

Part V: Supporting Audit Processes

Corrective and Preventive Action Influence (ISO 9001:2000 Sections 8.5.2, 8.5.3)

List and briefly describe any prior nonconformance and/or corrective actions to determine effectiveness *(within the audited process)*.

Non-Conformance #	*Vendor*	*Situation*	*VCA Completed OK ?*
#1157	ABC Vendor	Broken railcar seal	Yes
#1775	XYZ Vendor	Split wood received	Yes–in process
#1823	123 Vendor	Contaminated resin received	Yes– Material replaced by vendor

List and describe any preventive actions to investigate during the audit.

*Railcar fall protection for processing/inspecting railcars found to be in place and working effectively. See **Preventive Action # 4665**.*

*NOTE: During the audit process, the audit team noticed that all members of Production Department were wearing their safety glasses. **Preventive Action # 4972**.*

Prior Audit(s) Influence (ISO 9001:2000 Sections 5.6, 8.2.2)

How did prior audits or Management Review contribute to this audit?

*Interviewed J Martens: **Annual Purchasing Audits for 2002 and 2003** showed no findings. Management Review for past 2 years shows no specific Purchasing Initiatives for follow-up.*

Written Processes Supporting the Audit Itself:
Purchasing Process–Online
NPP Quality Policy Manual–Revision E
RECS 100.doc–Quality Records

Part VI: Audit Summary

Audit of: Purchasing

Closing Comments, Insights and Suggestions, Findings, and Recommendations:

General:

The Purchasing Process was found to be in excellent shape. V.P. of Purchasing and staff members knew their system thoroughly and were able to answer all questions easily. The system has many methods for reporting its progress and performance. As such, Purchasing is very much an open activity within NPP. The fact that Keith Lindsay writes and reports Purchasing information at Monthly Managers' Meetings indicates a high degree of trust and responsibility between Jeff Martens and his staff.

Observations:

Approvals and full descriptions for some purchased items are managed in nonstandard ways. This practice is at odds with documented Purchasing procedures (7.4.2(a)). Solution may be as simple as adding a comment to the form or minor modification to the Purchasing procedures.

Findings:

None

Audit Team Signatures:

Jerry Delaine,   *Marcy Edwards,*   *Juan Gonzales,*
Production   *Office*   *Shipping*

Opening Meeting Date: June 23, 2004

Closing Meeting Date: June 29, 2004

Attendees Sign-In Sheet(s) Attached

Evidence indicated by items **underlined and in bold**.

Glossary

accountability—The willingness to accept responsibility. A person who is accountable takes full responsibility and ownership of the outcome.

eight management principles—The eight principles upon which the ISO 9000 series of quality standards is founded: customer focus; leadership; the involvement of people; the process approach; a systems approach to management; continuous improvement; a factual approach to decision making; and mutually beneficial supplier relationships.

finding—Information uncovered during an investigation. Theoretically, a finding can be either good or bad news; in practice, however, a finding is most often the discovery of a significant breakdown or omission of a process within the QMS.

global—A quality or condition that applies to all.

local—A quality or condition that applies to something specific.

objective evidence—Records, controlled documentation, meeting minutes, test logs, and other accounts of actions taken within the system and usually attached to the full audit report.

observation—A reported inaccuracy within an otherwise functioning process or system.

paraphrase—To summarize or repeat what the interviewee has said. Paraphrasing is effective for determining whether you've truly understood what was told to you.

process—The use of controlled resources to transform inputs into outputs.

QMS—Acronym for *quality management system,* an interconnected series of processes that work together to produce mutual value for an organization and its customers.

suboptimal—Literally, "less than the best." When performance is suboptimal, there is room for improvement.

suggestion—A comment that is included in the executive summary as a possible improvement to the audited process or system.

system—An interconnected group of processes designed to achieve a common goal or objective.

theory of constraints—A theory whereby all organizations have one or more processes that ultimately control (constrain) the speed or output of the entire system.

verification—Making sure that a something is as it should be. Verifying is a check function—for example, when an auditor verifies that a previous nonconformance is indeed corrected.

Index